HOW TO HIDE

A Practical Guide to Vanishing and Taking Your Assets with You

David Wilkening

HOW TO HIDE: A PRACTICAL GUIDE TO VANISHING AND TAKING YOUR ASSETS WITH YOU

1405 SW 6th Avenue • Ocala, Florida 34471 • Phone 800-814-1132 • Fax 352-622-1875
Web site: www.atlantic-pub.com • E-mail: sales@atlantic-pub.com
SAN Number: 268-1250

Library of Congress Cataloging-in-Publication Data

Wilkening, David, 1943-
How to hide : a practical guide to vanishing and taking your assets with you / by David Wilkening.
p. cm.
Includes bibliographical references and index.
ISBN-13: 978-1-60138-309-9 (alk. paper)
ISBN-10: 1-60138-309-6 (alk. paper)
1. Missing persons--United States. 2. Identification--Miscellanea. 3. Identity (Psychology) I. Title.
HV6762.A3W535 2010
646.7--dc22
2010007122

PROJECT MANAGER: Melissa Peterson • INTERIOR DESIGN: Samantha Martin
FRONT & BACK COVER DESIGN: Jackie Miller • millerjackiej@gmail.com

Printed on Recycled Paper

Printed in the United States

We recently lost our beloved pet "Bear," who was not only our best and dearest friend but also the "Vice President of Sunshine" here at Atlantic Publishing. He did not receive a salary but worked tirelessly 24 hours a day to please his parents. Bear was a rescue dog that turned around and showered myself, my wife, Sherri, his grandparents Jean, Bob, and Nancy, and every person and animal he met (maybe not rabbits) with friendship and love. He made a lot of people smile every day.

We wanted you to know that a portion of the profits of this book will be donated to The Humane Society of the United States. ***–Douglas & Sherri Brown***

The human-animal bond is as old as human history. We cherish our animal companions for their unconditional affection and acceptance. We feel a thrill when we glimpse wild creatures in their natural habitat or in our own backyard.

Unfortunately, the human-animal bond has at times been weakened. Humans have exploited some animal species to the point of extinction.

The Humane Society of the United States makes a difference in the lives of animals here at home and worldwide. The HSUS is dedicated to creating a world where our relationship with animals is guided by compassion. We seek a truly humane society in which animals are respected for their intrinsic value, and where the human-animal bond is strong.

Want to help animals? We have plenty of suggestions. Adopt a pet from a local shelter, join The Humane Society and be a part of our work to help companion animals and wildlife. You will be funding our educational, legislative, investigative and outreach projects in the U.S. and across the globe.

Or perhaps you'd like to make a memorial donation in honor of a pet, friend or relative? You can through our Kindred Spirits program. And if you'd like to contribute in a more structured way, our Planned Giving Office has suggestions about estate planning, annuities, and even gifts of stock that avoid capital gains taxes.

Maybe you have land that you would like to preserve as a lasting habitat for wildlife. Our Wildlife Land Trust can help you. Perhaps the land you want to share is a backyard—that's enough. Our Urban Wildlife Sanctuary Program will show you how to create a habitat for your wild neighbors.

So you see, it's easy to help animals. And The HSUS is here to help.

THE HUMANE SOCIETY OF THE UNITED STATES

2100 L Street NW • Washington, DC 20037 • 202-452-1100
www.hsus.org

GPS
Options

dedication

To my parents, Margaret and Vernon Wilkening…
who were always there.

table of contents

publisher's preface

Why a person would choose to start a new life may seem foreign to some, but for many people who are perhaps involved in an abusive relationship or were victims of or witnesses to a violent crime, the idea of escaping to a safe haven can be very appealing. These are just a few reasons why a person would want to escape into new identity, but there are many. In this book, you will find many examples of ways to establish and protect your new life.

Hiding your assets probably conjures images of criminals and fraudulent activity. However, as you can see from the examples above, there are many legal reasons for someone to want to hide from a threatening situation. Many people who read this book may just be curious about changing their identity. Perhaps you are a person in a witness protection program who still feels vulnerable and would like more ideas on protecting your new identity.

Whatever your reason is for picking up this book, we hope that you find it engaging and informative. Please remember that we are in no way attorneys or accountants, and that we always recommend consulting with a legal or tax professional before adhering to advice, suggestions, or techniques in this book. We also are not recommending you take part in any illegal activity. Throughout the book, you will see many places where it is suggested that you consult with a legal or tax professional on a specific matter. Please do so before taking the advice offered in this book.

We also believe that running from an emotional situation may not be the best course of action. Please note that there are many victims' advocacy support programs throughout the United States. It is always in your best interest to seek the guidance and support of such a group before taking matters into your own hands. You can find information on support groups, including their telephone numbers, addresses, e-mail addresses, and Web sites, in Chapter 1 of this book.

Thank you for picking up *How to Hide*. We wish you much success on whichever path your life leads you.

chapter 1

Why Do You Want to Disappear?

If you are contemplating leaving your current life in favor of a fresh start, you are undoubtedly dealing with extremely difficult circumstances. Many people dealing with this predicament decide to simply pack up their things and leave without a moment's notice. They suddenly reach a mental breaking point in which they can no longer deal with their difficult situation, whatever it might be. Before you reach this breaking point, explore the first two chapters of this book to make sure disappearing is the best solution to your problems. Feeling trapped in an unwanted situation can cloud your mind and lead to decisions that only make life harder.

Vanishing is not easy, and it does not guarantee your problems will go away. Magicians make assistants disappear all the time, but no matter how convincing the illusion is, the audience knows he or she is still somewhere nearby. The illusion is considered magical because it is impossible to simply disappear out of thin air. If you decide to leave your current life, you must understand the process will be far from magical. Assuming a new identity presents more formidable challenges than the dazzling tricks of a magician.

Perhaps the toughest of these challenges is leaving behind loved ones. The isolation from one's family, friends, work colleagues, and neighbors may create an unbearable loneliness. On the other hand, if you are someone seeking refuge from an abusive spouse or have been a victim or witness of a crime, disappearing may seem like a completely sensible solution to consider.

This book is not for people trying to flee from the law. People attempting to hide from legal prosecution usually find their new life is just as unstable as the old one. Also, they must carry the burden of a guilty conscience and live in fear of being discovered. Those seeking to evade the law are also more likely to be found, as police are much more interested in finding fugitives rather than someone who chooses to disappear.

Some private investigators, such as John Hansen, are very skilled at finding those who stage their own disappearance. The following is a Case Study that shows how he went about tracking down a man engaged in criminal activity.

CASE STUDY: THE CASE OF THE MISSING PASTOR

John Hansen
Licensed Private Investigator

CLASSIFIED CASE STUDIES™ directly from the experts

John Hansen is a retired Bellevue, Wash., police detective with private investigative offices in Seattle and Phoenix.

In late 2000, I received a call from the assistant pastor of a small rural church in an area east of Seattle who asked if I could meet with him and the board of elders about their senior pastor, who had been missing for five days. The missing pastor was 56, married with three adult children who were also married and in the ministry. The missing clergyman had been pastor of the church for about 20 years.

In a note to the elders and staff, the pastor said any attempts to find him would be futile. In another note left at the church for his wife, the man of the cloth said he had been "living a lie" for many years and could stand it no more. He left her enough cash to live on for a few months, and expressed his affection for, and regrets to, his children.

Before leaving, the pastor had erased the hard drive of his computer and left a pile of shredded papers. We took the computer as evidence and handed it over to a retrieval company, and I gave the shredded papers to one of our investigators to reconstruct. Recent photographs of him showed that he had grown a full beard in the previous year.

The pastor's wife told me her home phone caller ID indicated he had called her from the immediate vicinity of Sea-Tac International Airport. We found the call was made from a pay phone in a bar across Highway 99 from the airport. I suspected the pastor wanted to mislead others into believing he had taken a plane to faraway places. I figured he had done just the opposite, and was still in the area.

From the pastor's desk drawers, we found credit card and checking account evidence that the fugitive had taken out about ⅓ of his paycheck in cash for the last 18 months. A thorough check of his home and office trash yielded no evidence of a new or secret checking account or credit card. These indications of long-range planning and intent showed that the pastor led a double life and had prepared for quick escape if exposed.

The case became fleshed out a bit when we learned from members that the pastor seemed to have a romantic interest in a married woman in the congregation. It had become obvious to church members he couldn't take his eyes off her while preaching Sunday sermons. The woman's husband — her fifth — said she had recently divorced him, and that she denied any interest in the pastor. He said that, several times after the divorce, he had seen his car and hers parked at the church late at night.

The ex-husband believed, as did the elders and the church members we interviewed, that the woman's employer had transferred her to company headquarters in St. Joseph, Mo. The church had even thrown a going-away party for her.

I called the Seattle office of the woman's employer and was informed they never had an office in Missouri. A female investigator on our staff called the payroll office of the woman's employer and, posing as the woman, asked to check the mailing address they had for her. The payroll office gave an address in Everett, north of Seattle.

I arrived at the Everett trailer park where the woman lived with four investigators, and we discovered the pastor's car parked outside one of the trailers with new and different license plates. On the way to the trailer park, I had received a call from the computer recovery firm informing me that they had recovered hard-core child pornography on the pastor's computer and they had already called the police.

When we arrived at the trailer park, we set up a perimeter of surveillance units and, within an hour, we observed the woman arrive in her car, evidently from work. Minutes later, we saw her and the pastor, who was now clean-shaven, walking hand-in-hand. We notified the church elders that we had found the pastor, and they soon arrived on the scene with the pastor's children. However, the clergyman refused to meet or talk with his children.

When the police arrived, we left because our case was closed. We later learned that the pastor and his female friend were involved with an international child pornography ring based in Texas. Raids on U.S. locations related to the ring had started a week before the pastor "disappeared."

Running from Your Problems

The general public often assumes adults who choose to disappear are criminals, but often that is not the case. Most are just desperate to escape the turmoil of their everyday lives. Whatever your reason, seek help before abandoning your life. There are countless organizations in the United States that want to help people get their lives back together. Even if you are certain no one can help fix your situation, these outreach organizations may still be able to provide support after you flee.

If you are overwhelmed by the countless stressful burdens life throws your way, many professionals in the mental health field suggest taking a time out. Take a break and get away from everything for a day or two. Clear your head and rationally evaluate your situation. When you distance yourself from your problems, obvious solutions may suddenly appear. A change from your everyday routine often helps you sort your problems out.

Deciding to disappear is not a crime unless there are extenuating circumstances, such as skipping out on debtors, leaving to avoid legal charges, or stealing someone else's identity. The choice to disappear is not always easy to understand, particularly because it can cause such pain to those left behind, but it is worth repeating: *It is not a crime in itself to disappear.*

Why people leave is often a mystery to those left behind, but it is more common than most people think. In some countries, such as Australia, the rate of missing persons is higher than road traffic accidental deaths and suicide combined, according to the Attorney General's Department of New South Wales.

Professionals have developed a profile for missing people. According to one small study, nearly 50 percent of participants were suffering from some form of mental illness, and another 16 percent were suspected of having suicidal tendencies.

Another study found the biggest reason for leaving was relationship break-ups, which accounted for almost 33 percent, followed by conflicts for independence, particularly among younger people. The following is a list of reasons for disappearing, in descending order of frequency:

1. To escape a crisis or ongoing stress
2. Mental health problems, such as depression
3. Alcohol abuse
4. Financial problems
5. Job loss
6. Domestic violence
7. Transient lifestyles.

The following sections provide additional details about a few of the reasons why some people might decide to disappear.

CASE STUDY: FLEEING FROM BUSINESS PRESSURES IN THE UNITED STATES

Janice Sellers

CLASSIFIED CASE STUDIES™ directly from the experts

Janice Sellers is a resident of Oakland, Calif., where she currently works as the office manager for a day care center.

This story came to my attention through friends who operate a storage warehouse and asked me to help them clear out abandoned stock and correspondence of a company known as Puff the Magic Dragon's Treasure Trove, a wholesaler to the adventure games industry. In the process of helping them, I ran across paperwork from the business indicating that the owner, Johnny

Drake, was delinquent on practically every bill, even though his business was quite successful at first.

Although initially successful, the company grew too quickly for Drake to get a handle on the necessary administrative tasks. He continued to take in product and make sales, but got extremely behind on all payments to vendors, the U.S. government, state government, and other creditors. He also was not able to keep up with shipping the sales he had made and was getting dunning letters from vendors and threats from governmental agencies.

For some reason, Drake refused to take any advice on how to deal with the situation and eventually stopped responding to phone calls and email messages. He sold a considerable amount of his product (games), arranged to move the remaining product into a friend's house, and agreed to pay them a monthly storage fee — and then disappeared!

No one heard from him for several months, and then he sent an e-mail to my friends who worked at the warehouse telling them he had moved to New Zealand. He holds dual U.S./New Zealand citizenship and his mother is from New Zealand. Drake paid storage fees for a couple of months, and then stopped responding to his prior e-mail address. As far as I know, none of his friends or former business associates has heard from him since his "disappearance" in 2004.

Drake left behind games and books he had been selling — much of the product was not his. He had been warehousing it for several companies that had no idea what had happened to their product when Drake dropped out of sight. An important part of my job was returning stored items to their rightful owners.

The only news we have heard about Drake since he left is second-hand. A friend who lives in Australia told me that a friend of hers happened to run into Drake at a convention in Sydney. Apparently, Drake was extremely shocked to discover anyone in Australia would recognize him because he left quite suddenly.

I knew many of Drake's friends and professional acquaintances, including vendors. They could not understand why he decided to take such drastic action. Most of us felt the situation was salvageable, if he had been willing to work at it. His vendors felt betrayed because he left owing a lot of money to many people.

> For the first few years after his disappearance, the mere mention of his name would incite very irate reactions. Even now, some people get upset thinking about what happened, but most people wrote off the bad debt and moved on.

Abuse

No one should have to suffer at the hands of an abuser whether the abuse is physical, emotional, or both. If this is your case, you may feel like no one can help you. Abusers are often controlling and may limit or completely remove your ability to contact your family and friends. However, if you have managed to get a copy of this book, you are on the right path. You will learn how to disappear, so your abuser cannot find you, and then seek the support of the abundance of resources available to victims of abuse. Specific notes are added throughout this book to help conceal plans to leave, as well as what to do if children are involved.

Abuse situations can arise in any living condition and between any two people. According to the National Coalition Against Domestic Violence, one in four women will experience domestic violence during her lifetime and 85 percent of domestic violence victims are women. There are, however, other abusive relationships that often go unnoticed. Women also abuse their husbands and boyfriends, parents abuse grown children, and teenagers abuse parents. Sadly, society feels the abused in these situations should be able to fix their problems. For example, husbands are stereotyped as being stronger than their wives, so they should be able to easily defend themselves. Victims in these situations feel even more hopeless.

Resources for Victims of Abuse

National Coalition Against Domestic Violence

www.ncadv.org
Phone: (303) 839-1852

Although this organization focuses on abused women and children, it seeks to expand its scope and help make "every home a safe home."

SAFE (Stop Abuse For Everyone)

www.safe4all.org
Phone: (503) 853-8686

SAFE is a smaller organization, but it is focused on the diverse relationships that can be abusive and have little support, which includes homosexual relationships, abused men, teenagers, and the elderly.

National Center for Victims of Crime

www.ncvc.org
Phone: 1-800-FYI-CALL (1-800-394-2255)

The NCVC provides general victim assistance. Those who are abused, stalked, or need to file a civil case will all find emotional and legal help here.

The Family Violence Prevention Fund

www.endabuse.org
Phone: (415) 252-8900

This organization originally focused on helping women and children, but it is now working to extend help to teenagers and men, as well as anyone else who is a victim of violence. It focuses on creating a society that is violence free, not just on individual homes.

Emerge

www.emergedv.com
Phone: (617) 547-9879

Emerge not only seeks to educate those who are abused, but helps the abuser learn to change his or her behavior. Although the group meetings are only advantageous to those who live in Cambridge, Mass., where the organization is based, there is still good information on the Web site.

The National Domestic Violence Hotline

www.ndvh.org
Phone: 1-800-799-SAFE (7233) or 1-800-787-3224

Established as a component of the Violence Against Women Act passed by Congress in 1996. The non-profit hotline provides crisis intervention, information, and referrals to victims of domestic violence. The hotline is available 24 hours a day, 365 days a year.

CASE STUDY: HOW AND WHY BATTERED WOMEN 'DISAPPEAR'

Dr. Will Marling

CLASSIFIED CASE STUDIES™
directly from the experts

Dr. Will Marling is executive director of the National Organization for Victim Assistance® (NOVA) based in Washington, D.C.

Domestic violence is a crisis of staggering proportions. Approximately 50 percent of the victim assistance resources in the United States are spent on domestic violence. Society is prone to judge women who seemingly will not leave abusive relationships. However, the complexities of these situations are not just emotional, but also financial and social, complicating the problem to the point these women are not able to leave easily.

Statistics show that women are the victims of domestic violence in 85 percent of cases. One major challenge such women face is escaping the control of their abuser. The typical abuser profile includes some level of narcissistic control based on threats and intimidation, to maintain power in the relationship.

There are legal instruments available to such women, like protection orders. However, legal protection orders are simply papers that do not guarantee safety and security. It is like a piece of paper trying to stop a bullet. In a large number of these situations, women do not just need to escape. They also need to disappear, at least from their abusers.

Disappearing is difficult. Batterers typically control finances and legal documents — two essential components of breaking free of the abuser's shackles. Some women are able to go into hiding, but my own experience demonstrates that the long-term effectiveness of that strategy is limited.

Victims of domestic violence may have children to protect, and even though divorced the abuser may have court-ordered access to those children and the woman cannot leave the area. The contexts for successful disappearance of a domestic violence victim depend to some extent on the ingenuity of the battered woman who has decided she will be smarter and more strategic than her abuser, operative law enforcement and justice system involvement, support of family and friends and sheer determination of the victim to survive.

Depression and anxiety

Those who suffer from depression and anxiety feel like the world is closing in around them and they have to escape. Some are not even aware they are depressed, so if you feel hopeless and that is why you desire to escape to a new life, find out if you are suffering from depression or anxiety. There are numerous online tests that will help you identify possible symptoms. You should also consult a doctor to find out if you are depressed before deciding to run away. It would be a shame to run away and leave loved ones, which will only make you feel worse down the road. Running away is a quick fix, but the underlying problems must be healed, or the condition will only return in your new life.

Resources for Readers with Depression or Anxiety

Find the Light

www.findthelight.net

An online support forum for those suffering from various mood disorders, anxiety, and substance abuse, as substance abuse is a method of self-medicating a mood disorder.

Stress Anxiety and Depression Resource Center **www.stress-anxiety-depression.org** A Web site that encourages the healing of stress, anxiety, and depression through researching different treatment methods.
Anxiety Disorders Association of America **www.adaa.org** An organization that helps people suffering from anxiety disorders, such as post-traumatic stress syndrome, obsessive-compulsive behavior, panic disorder, and phobias.
National Hopeline Network **www.hopeline.com** 1-800-SUICIDE (1-800-784-2433) The Kristin Brooks Hope Center has many programs to help prevent suicide, mainly the National Hopeline. The center is extremely active and involved and a great resource.

Debt

While running away from overwhelming debt is illegal, it is an appealing choice for many people with financial burdens. The pressure of owing so much money can consume your thoughts and leave no room for anything else in life. No one can be expected to deal with that kind of pressure, but running away will only cause more problems. The creditors you owe money to have many ways of tracking individuals and will put as much effort as possible into retrieving their money. This book is not meant to help you flee debt. There are practical ways to fix monetary problems that will not destroy your life, and you may even be able to salvage your credit. Money does not have to control your life, and you are far from alone in your situation. Creditors will take your willingness to get out of debt as a positive sign and do all they can to encourage payment, such as reduced or suspended APR, postponed payments, and overall debt reduction.

Resources for Readers Handling Debt Issues
Federal Trade Commission **www.ftc.gov/bcp/edu/pubs/consumer/credit/cre19.shtm** This portion of the FTC Web site offers the best advice for those who are "Knee Deep in Debt". There are countless organizations that claim to help those in debt, but the FTC lists the qualities to be wary of as not all of the organizations have good intentions.

Illness

Many people who have serious or terminal illnesses feel they are a burden to loved ones and would be doing them a favor if they just disappeared. Although illness can put a deep strain on a family, it does not mean that the ill person is unloved. Yes, high medical expenses and extensive time caring for the ill person can create burdens, but if that person disappears, the family is left with the heavier burden of the loss of a loved one. If you are ill, you cannot alleviate your family's burden by leaving. You do not want to be sick, and they know that.

Resources for Readers Combating Serious Illness
Care for the Family **www.careforthefamily.org.uk/supportnet** The support section of Care for the Family includes a section on families dealing with a seriously ill family member as well as numerous other family scenarios such as the loss of a child, eating disorders, and divorce.
APA Help Center **http://www.apa.org/helpcenter/** The American Physiological Association has many articles about emotional and physical health and well-being.

The Consequences of Leaving

As the previous scenarios mention, it is clear that help is available. Leaving your life behind is not the only option. However, perhaps you still feel the need to disappear for a period of time to remain safe. If so, the remainder of this book will assist you in this endeavor.

Your disappearance will affect people. You may feel alone, but everyone is loved by someone. Think about how disappearing will affect others, especially those you care most about. Do you really want to put them through the pain of not knowing where you are, and whether you are safe and happy? The consequences of disappearing can affect you and those in your life, so even if it seems to solve personal problems, you may be creating new problems for those closest to you.

This is a huge decision. It will define the rest of your life. If people are looking for you, it is natural to constantly look over your shoulder and worry about being found. If you decide to return to your old life after disappearing, even after a short period of absence, nothing will be the same. Family and friends will worry you may leave again and may constantly keep tabs on your actions and whereabouts.

How will you be affected?

Even if you decide that running away is your best option to solve your problems, you must realize that it is not a foolproof strategy. Disappearing can affect you in several ways.

One of the major reasons you might decide to disappear is to find a peace and happiness you feel is unattainable in your current life, but not everyone is able to achieve this goal with a fresh start. It is impossible to tell whether these people are happy with their decision to create a new life for themselves because people who choose to disappear have no contact with those they leave behind. Various estimates range from 10 to 90 percent. This is a broad statistic, but the bottom line is that everyone is not happy with his or her new life.

Even if you are lucky enough to find happiness in your escape, it might not be for long. According to a study from the National Missing Persons Coordination Centre in Australia, 99.5 percent of those who left were located, often within one month of their disappearance. That number gives credence to the old saying that people cannot run away to escape their problems, as new identities can create concerns just as disturbing as the old ones. *Please refer to the Appendix for more information on support groups and alternatives to leaving.*

Missing persons are a worldwide concern. In the United States, there are as many as 100,000 active missing persons cases on any given day. According to the National Institute of Justice, tens of thousands of people disappear under suspicious circumstances. In Australia, approximately 30,000 people go missing for various reasons every year. The most common reasons for disappearing are family and financial problems. If you are dealing with these kind of problems, you should try to solve them before resorting to running away from them.

If your situation involves fraud or skipping out on creditors, you have additional concerns to take into account when making your decision. Avoiding a financial situation will create strong motivation for investigators to find you. Committing fraud or evasion is illegal. Professionals will be on your case, and they are not easily discouraged. In recent years, creditors, aided by new technology, have stepped up efforts to find debtors in a stronger push to collect. If you owe a large sum, the best solution is to work the problem out, perhaps by making manageable payments on debt.

Before embarking on a new life, try to imagine what it will be like. Hypothetically, assume you have successfully gone through the elaborate steps of getting a new identity. Suppose you used to enjoy getting out on weekends and working in the yard. You will certainly want to avoid doing that because it might lead to some neighborhood friendships. Friends want to know about you, but discussing the past will be incredibly difficult.

You will be unable to tell anyone this major secret of your life. Not a new love interest, a friend, or even relatives — no one. All it would take to blow the lid off your cover would be an angry lover or a talkative friend who enjoys sharing secrets.

If you are leaving behind a family, perhaps you have been planning to replace it with many newfound friends. This is a bad idea because it is easy to trip up when you have to invent stories about your past. The more people you tell your story, the harder it will be to keep the facts straight. If you begin to make mistakes or give contradictory information, such as telling someone you hail from one hometown when you told others you came from somewhere else, friends begin to wonder and question you further.

You also must realize that in the first days of freedom, you will be homesick. You will have to overcome these natural feelings because you cannot write or call relatives. If anyone is looking for you, those are among the first people who will be contacted.

Before deciding there is no alternative to leaving, carefully consider what you will be giving up, beginning with your spouse. Many people leave because of finances or personal problems, such as a spouse whose love has been lost.

Children also have to be considered. Someone eager to leave has to consider whether they will ever see their children again or watch them grow up. In addition to family, decide whether you can suddenly cut off relationships with friends and face the prospect of not having future relationships.

How will your loved ones be affected?

Solving problems, whatever they may be, may seem like an overwhelming job. However, before disappearing, consider the guilt you will feel over the suffering of those you leave behind. You may be dealing with serious problems, but those left behind also suffer immensely, as documented by various self-help groups for families of missing persons. The following are some potential problems that may be encountered by loved ones who are abandoned:

- Many families and friends of those left behind experience negative health effects, which are often a direct result of abandonment, and any pre-existing health conditions will likely be worsened.

- Long-term health effects not immediately apparent can also crop up. The stress and trauma often experienced by those missing a loved one can affect their body's ability to resist or withstand even minor illnesses, such as colds.

- Self-help groups for families of missing people report employment problems as well. The loved ones back home often take time off from work to look for a missing person. They often have trouble concentrating while at work.

- Searching for someone who is missing takes time, effort, and energy. The entire quality of life of those left behind can be impacted and can lead to reduced involvement in social and leisure activities.

- There can be serious financial consequences. Families often spend money to hire investigators to find a missing loved one. There may also be a loss in earnings, health-related costs, legal fees, and even property losses.

- The disappearance of a loved one can also affect the mental health of those who are abandoned. That might lead to many problems, such as nightmares, a poor attention span, difficulties in making decisions and concentrating, and broad disorientation.

- Even if you decide to return, you will find there are serious emotional issues to overcome, including trust, anger, and hurt feelings of those you left behind.

Put yourself in the place of those you would leave behind. Your loved ones would have no proof of whether you are alive or not.

Many spend years, and sometimes their life savings, in a futile search to find missing loved ones.

Even if the missing person decides to return voluntarily, his or her loved ones are forever affected by the decision. Estimates say, for every missing person, 12 people suffer consequences.

The suffering can occur in many forms. Some family members may take time off from work to locate the missing person or deal with the emotional stress of not knowing what happened to their missing loved one. This complicates the already difficult financial situation that arises after a disappearance, especially because many of those who disappear were the primary source of income for their family. Not to mention, everyday family routines are disrupted in a person's absence.

Additionally, a variety of mental health problems can arise after a loved one disappears. Anxiety and depression are common emotions for those left behind, particularly if the relationship was strained before the sudden departure. A person's disappearance leaves a lot of uncertainty behind because so many questions cannot be answered, so it can be very hard for those left behind to accept the reality of the situation.

Families also face bureaucratic nightmares because it can take years for someone to be declared officially dead or absent. Meanwhile, family members may be unable to claim their inheritance, sell property, remarry, or simply hold funeral rites.

Your family members will have to go through a lengthy process before you are declared dead so they can clear up those issues. Most states have a statute in which a person can only be declared dead if no contact is made within seven years. But that is only the beginning of the process. A spouse or immediate family has to petition the court, and there are various legal obstacles he or she has to overcome depending on the state. Sometimes it has to be proven that the person is dead, which is not easy to do without evidence.

Most states will recognize a disappearance as a death as long as a person has been missing for at least seven years and the absence has been continuous and without explanation. Additionally, persons likely to have communication with the missing must have heard nothing during those seven years. In some cases, states will lower the time element from seven to five years, or even less.

A declaration of death can provide closure for family members. It sometimes allows people who have been left behind by loved ones that have disappeared more of an opportunity to move on with their lives. Without this declaration, family members face a challenge to move on because there is no closure. A person who disappears usually leaves behind a life situation that goes into a state of limbo or suspense. In some ways, your death may have been a less-complicated outcome for the loved ones involved.

chapter 2

Planning Your Disappearance

If you choose to leave your life behind, you will have to create a new life with a new identity. You will have to leave the "old" person behind and willing to do whatever it takes to disappear, as long as it is legal. That means discarding old family members and friends, perhaps even your spouse and children. By completely discarding your old life, you will need to:

- Thwart the resources of anyone trying to find you.
- Cope with the reality that you are running from your old life.
- Understand you will be hiding out from those who might want to find you.
- Legally acquire a new personhood with new identification because it is against the law to lie about social security numbers and other identification.
- Continue to pay taxes.

- Have medical and other insurance, just in case things go wrong.
- Learn to be suspicious of everyone you encounter in your new life.
- Give up the way of life you have grown accustomed to.

Your disappearance comes at a cost, and you will quickly see that creating a new life is not easy. You must decide whether you are willing to pay that price.

It would be nice and easy if you could just pack your bags, take your money out of the bank, and flee to a better destination. Unfortunately, that route is out of the question. Planning is an absolute necessity if you do not want to be found. Give yourself anywhere from six months to one year, depending on how much free time is available.

Before leaving, it is necessary to prepare. Here are 11 important steps you need to take when preparing to disappear. Some of these may take time, so it is best to start early.

1. **Start to cut personal ties with friends and acquaintances.** Gradually drop out of all groups and organizations. Do this slowly though, so others will not notice or become suspicious. This can take several months, depending on how active you are in the community. If your absence would draw too much attention, continue to go. You do not want to raise any flags by changing your behavior too drastically.

2. **Delete every online account that you do not need.** People paid bills and purchased goods before the Internet, and you

can too. Many people who tried to disappear were caught because of updated contact information with a company. If you plan to get a new name and identity, you are going to have to recreate these accounts anyway, so you might as well delete them.

3. **Start creating misinformation concerning all of your contact information.** Tell companies you have accounts with that you need to update your information and give them a fake phone number. Forward all bills to post office boxes in other states and then call the utility company and pay over the phone with a prepaid credit card.

4. **Stop any actions that add to public records.** This includes driver's licenses, auto registrations, property ownership records, voter registration cards, marriage license certificates, business filings, and even hunter or angler licenses. Many individuals who thought they successfully relocated were tripped up when they applied for licenses to hunt bear or catch trout. Some of those permits are limited, allowing investigators to quickly find you. When you leave, you need to get rid of all these documents.

5. **Liquidate assets and pay off debts.** Rid yourself of all stocks, property, and even possessions, except for a week or two of clothing. Meet with a financial advisor or tax accountant before taking these steps to make sure that you address any legal issues.

6. **Close bank accounts and prepay for things whenever possible.** Paying with credit and debit cards creates a record

that investigators can use to see your location and time of purchase.

7. **Sell or relinquish all ties to your living arrangements.** If you rent, you should have no problem leaving. You may be required to pay early-termination fees on a rental agreement. Look over your lease in order to abide by all contractual agreements. On the other hand, if you own a house or condominium, you will have to sell it. Depending on the housing market, this can take weeks or even months. If you are fleeing from someone you live with, you will just have to abandon the property.

8. **Sell your vehicle, if you own one**. It would be best if you can sell it in the name of your own identity and receive cash in exchange. You can also accept a check because the buyer will most likely not know your address, except for the one that is currently listed on the title, which will be incorrect once you leave. Be very careful when selling your car that there is nothing left behind revealing anything about your new life and identity. Also, make sure you abide by any necessary legal provisions required by law when selling your car.

9. **If you plan to reinvent yourself, change the details of your life story.** Be boring. Although it is not much fun, anything interesting or special will only make you worth remembering and can trap you in a lie during a conversation when someone asks for details you did not anticipate. If you really need to get away from an old identity, start doing

some intense research or even go back to school to make your story more believable.

10. **Research tips on how to create a believable fiction character.** This will provide a framework for inventing your new identity. Simply typing "how to create believable characters" into a search engine will provide a slew of information to look over. Do this at an Internet café or on someone else's computer. Once you establish your new identity, you can then gain new interests and develop into a completely new person.

11. **In the week before departure, continue to make a point of seeing all your close friends.** This is important so that people close to you do not become suspicious. If they ask where you have been, you can give a vague answer about working or being busy with family.

Hide Your Plans to Disappear

You need to keep plans to leave a secret and prevent anyone from stumbling across information that could reveal your intentions. This is especially true if you live with someone who is abusive. Do not change your normal behavior. This is a big tip-off, and people notice more than you may think. Do not get so absorbed in yourself that you forget you are not gone yet.

Be cautious about writing down any information about your plans or research. Unless you can somehow keep all papers in your possession or secure 24 hours a day, someone could find them.

If you are leaving in a hurry, hide emergency cash, clothing, and important documents that you can access easily and quickly.

If you live alone, get a safe to store everything in. If you live with someone else this will be more difficult. The worst places to hide anything in a home include closets, dresser drawers, night tables, under mattresses, inside old clothes, or jewelry boxes. These are the first points of interest for anyone interested in finding clues about your plans. A storage area outside your home is also not a good idea because access may not be available if it is needed quickly.

However, your home or apartment does provide many effective hiding places. If you have large flour bins in the kitchen, you ca hide your papers in bags buried under the flour. Another possibility is to take an old package of frozen food, put your papers inside and re-glue. Put the food back in the freezer. It is unlikely anyone will go to the trouble of opening all the frozen food packages when searching for clues of your disappearance.

Consider burying small items in the bottom of potted plants, concealed in waterproof plastic containers, such as small aspirin bottles. Additionally, it is possible to build secret compartments in sofas, end tables, chairs, or bookshelves.

Another possibility is to build a hollow area behind a portion of baseboard in your home. Baseboards are in every room of the house, so they are logical hiding places. Cutting away a small part of the drywall and making a hiding space that is covered with wallpaper will also work, as long as it is on a part of the wall no one is likely to touch.

A bookcase can also be a hiding place. Take a big, hardbound book and glue the pages together. Then cut out a rectangular section in the pages and store important things to be hidden. Glue this rectangular section to the back cover of the book.

There are also a number of "decoy" or "diversion" safes available, which look like common household items, such as fire extinguishers, smoke detectors, light switches, peanut butter jars, flowerpots, and lamps.

Floor safes are expensive, but they work best. You can put a floor safe beneath a sofa in the living room and cover it with a rug.

If you do not feel comfortable with hiding papers in the house, a yard has many storage options. One method is cache tubes. A cache tube is made with polyvinyl chloride, or PVC, drain tubing that has threaded end caps. Protect papers in plastic bags before placing them in the tubes then glue the end caps in place. PVC tubing is strong enough to withstand most natural elements, such as corrosives, salts, and water.

Another outdoor option is to hide things in the hollowed legs of patio furniture or even the legs of a child's swing set. Again, put your valuables in several layers of plastic bags.

Hide your computer information

Any online research you conduct, such as looking for a new place to live or what the laws are regarding changing your name, needs to be done on a public computer or a laptop only you have access to. It is virtually impossible to completely clear a computer of all information because of the countless ways computers are able to record information. Information stored in a computer's memory can lead to your whereabouts being figured out by an intelligent spouse or even a private investigator. There is a national directory of community technology centers at the Community Technology Centers' Network Web site (**www.ctcnet.org**) if finding a place to access a public computer is necessary. Remember, even access the Web site just listed will be traceable, so try to do as much research offline as possible. Almost everything you do online is traceable.

Secure your Web browser

You may not realize the browser, such as Firefox or Internet Explorer records a list of the Web sites you have visited on the Internet. You can turn these features off, but if you share the computer, the other person can easily notice these changes and turn them back on. If the other person only uses Firefox, but Internet Explorer is still on the computer, use that browser instead. The following offers directions for clearing your Internet history usage for various browsers:

- **Firefox:** Click "Tools" on the top bar of Firefox. Click "Clear Private Data" and choose what information to delete. There is even an option for Firefox to stop storing data from your browsing history – uncheck "Save information I enter in forms and the Search Bar."

- **Internet Explorer:** Close Internet Explorer and go to the computer's Control Panel. Click on "Internet Options" and then "Clear History," which is located on the "General" tab.

- **Safari:** Click "History" on the top bar of Safari. Click "Clear History" at the very bottom of the list. Safari also has an option called "Private Browsing," which you can find by clicking "Safari" on the top bar. This stops Safari from collecting a history of the Web pages you visit, anything you download will be automatically erased from the downloads window, nothing is added to the "Auto-Fill" feature, and new searches are not added to the search bar.

Delete your temporary Internet files

Temporary Internet files are stored to help load Web pages more quickly when revisiting. They are automatically collected with each visit to a Web site and, therefore, are also a record of every Web site you visit. You can manually delete them after each Internet session, or set the computer to automatically delete temporary files. To delete your temporary Internet files:

- **If you have a PC:** Go to the Control Panel and select "Internet Options." On the "General" tab, click "Delete Files," which is under the heading "Temporary Internet Files." Select the "Delete all offline content" option, and click OK. If you have many files, this will take a few minutes.

- **If you have a Mac:** Macs do not store temporary Internet files like PCs. Instead, clear the files by selecting "Empty Cache" in Safari. Just click "Safari" on the top bar and click "Empty Cache."

Search engine safety

Search engines record tons of information for the purpose of targeted advertising. The best option is to use a different search engine than anyone else who uses the computer, and to turn off certain features within the search engine.

Google is by far the most popular search engine, but it is very invasive. It has such advanced data collecting that every single keystroke can be recorded. Do you ever notice how Google always advertises things that are related to the things you search? That is not an accident. Google makes its profit by selling advertising space, and targeted ads generate more revenue for advertisers than random ads. It can scan your e-mails and find keywords that generate "relevant" ads along the sides, top, and bottom of your browser. This means anyone else using the same browser will see targeted ads and will become suspicious when there are numerous ads for travel or disappearing.

Opt out of targeted advertising in Google by going to **www.google.com/ads/preferences** and selecting to "opt out," but this only creates a cookie that will be deleted if you clear your temporary Internet files. To make this a permanent change, download the opt-out plug-in that appears to the right after initially selecting the opt-out option.

You will also need to turn off Google Suggestions. These are the suggestions that pop up below the search bar as you type. Google will remember old searches and re-suggest them, so someone could see what you last searched when they try to complete a search of their own. To disable this feature, click on "Search settings" on the top-right corner of Google. Then scroll down to the

"Query Suggestions" box, select "Do not provide query suggestions in the search box," and save your preferences.

Secure your e-mail

Although it is best to never e-mail any information about your plans, you may need to contact someone in another city while researching for a new place to live. Create a throwaway account that you only use for this purpose. There are plenty of free e-mail accounts available, so chose one that the other people in your home do not use. This will ensure they have no chance of accidentally logging into your e-mail or noticing your new screen name in the login area. A few of the more common sites include Gmail (**www.gmail.com**), Hotmail (**www.hotmail.com**), and Yahoo! (**www.mail.yahoo.com**).

A secure password is necessary to access e-mail. Never use obvious data in your password, such as initials, important dates, or the names of children or pets. The best passwords are random numbers and letters and, if possible, mix in capitalization and symbols. These may be difficult to remember, but it is the best protection against someone guessing your password. For even more security, change your password frequently. *See Chapter 8 for more information on creating a secure password.*

Do not rely on the computer to remember your password. This allows anyone who has access to your computer to automatically log into the e-mail account or any other Web site where you have stored a password. Instead, find a way to remember your password with a mnemonic device or another information recall strategy. A mnemonic device is something you say, do, or hear that reminds you of something else — like your password. Some common mnemonic devices are "Roy G. Biv," which is a name created from the first letters of all the colors of the rainbow (red, orange, yellow, green, blue, indigo, violet), or "Every Good Boy Does Fine" which is a sentence made from the letters of musical notes on the scale. Another option is to rewrite your password repeatedly, so your hand "remembers" the feeling of that specific combination of numbers and letters, but be sure to thoroughly dispose of the practice paper.

Always remember to log out of an e-mail account properly instead of just closing the browser. Many times just closing a browser leaves you logged into your account, and anyone who comes onto the computer after you can read your e-mail when he or she attempts to check his or her own account.

Save Your Money

If you have a steady job and an income, but share expenses with your spouse, it will be necessary to find ways of storing money somewhere else. Here are some suggestions:

- If you are already working and your spouse is accustomed to having you routinely share income, you will need to make excuses for not handing it over. The excuse should tailor to your situation and not tip off your spouse to any changes in behavior.

- If you are not employed, you can secretly work part-time, outside of the home. What kind of work you do is up to you, but it would be best to do something calling for talents your spouse did not know you had (just in case he or she starts looking for you and knows you have worked, for example, as an accountant).

- If your boss knows your situation, he or she might agree to cash your checks.

- If you need a job, register for free with an employment agency. Many of these agencies also offer job training to build skills.

- If time and money permit, enroll in classes at a local vocational school or community college.

- Another way to earn money without leaving your home is to put yourself on lists for volunteer surveys. Try CashCrate (**www.cashcrate.com**). You will not be making big money by expressing your opinion, but many surveys pay a few dollars. They pay by checks, and you can simply cash them at a check-cashing facility.

- If you do not want to do surveys, another low-income source of pay from home are sites such as Associated Content (**www.associatedcontent.com**) and Hubpages (**www.hubpages.com**). You can get paid small amounts by writing for these sites anonymously.

- Also, try to save money in a variety of small ways. If you have a grocery allowance, for example, buy less and save some cash for yourself. Collecting money in small amounts will eventually lead to larger sums.

- Do not throw away your wedding ring; pawn it instead. Do the same with other valuables you no longer want. Do this gradually, so you do not provide clues to your future plans.

- Do not leave your money with anyone – not even close family members.

- Store your money in a safe, safety deposit, or post office box. When you want it, it is there. The only disadvantage is that you have to carry around cash. Paying cash is a far better practice because using credit cards will leave a trace to help others find you.

- Safety deposit boxes limit your access to the bank's business hours, which may put a hitch in escape plans. Most post office boxes are more accessible, as post offices generally leave that part of the building unlocked, and often, it is accessible 24 hours a day.

- Another option is to put funds in a Web site, such as PayPal.

Get Copies of Your Vital Records

The Center for Disease Control hosts a Web site (**www.cdc.gov/nchs/w2w.htm**) that grants access to state Web sites and addresses you would need to obtain a copy of your birth, marriage, or divorce certificate.

You should also obtain copies of your medical records, which is usually as simple as signing a release form. Medical records help a doctor understand medical history so he or she can treat you properly in case of illness. Schedule a final exam before you plan to disappear just to be sure you are in good health. Also, update your contact information with the doctor by providing a fake address and phone number to create a false trail. Most doctors do little more than send out appointment reminders with this information anyway, and this may help to confuse an investigator if he or she thinks you may have provided accurate contact information.

If you have prescription medication, tell your doctor you are planning a vacation and ask for numerous refills, so you do not have to worry about running out.

If planning to move out of the country, particularly if you are considering a tropical climate, check immunization requirements or recommendations for any immunization. You can easily find information on the subject on the CDC Web site (**www.cdc.gov**).

Technology continues to jeopardize confidentiality, particularly in the medical field. Once records have been digitized, they can be sent without a trace all over the globe. Your entire medical and insurance history is now compiled online by an insurance industry database service called the American Index Bureau. Various agencies, such as the National Insurance Crime Bureau, collect medical and insurance claim records, which can be easily used to trace someone who tries to disappear.

Request FBI Information

Under the Freedom of Information Act initially enacted by Lyndon B. Johnson, as well as the Privacy Act of 1974, the American public has the right to access certain documents held in the FBI's Central Records System. This will likely not be of much use to many, but it may benefit you if you were involved in certain lawsuits or investigations, such as death threats or identity theft. Therefore, if you were a victim of identity theft, severe abuse, or stalking, and want to get a new social security number on these grounds, it will be helpful to have copies of the documents that prove your need for the request. You are the only non-government person that can request these documents without your permission, so anyone else wanting your information would have to get a notarized form signed by you that releases the information.

Send your FOIA request to:

Federal Bureau of Investigation
Record/Information Dissemination Section
170 Marcel Drive
Winchester, VA 22602-4843

The FBI will also release information they have on an organization, business, investigation, historical event, or incident. The request for this information can be sent electronically, and many of these documents are regularly released on the FBI's Web site. This would be useful to someone involved in or affected by federal cases against a business or organization rather than a single person. You should be able to access all of this information electronically after submitting the request.

If you were arrested at some point in your life and fingerprinted, the FBI will also release your records to you under the Privacy Act. The request costs $18 in certified check or money order form made out to the Treasurer of the United States. You must also mail in a copy of your fingerprints, which you can obtain at most UPS stores, or at a local courthouse. This information will be accessible to the police who will conduct your missing person search, so you might want to get a copy if you have any previous history. The police may think you are involved in more criminal activity due to your disappearance. Send your request, with the words "Privacy Act Request" written on both the envelope and enclosed request, to the same address as the FOIA request.

All of the forms, mailing instructions, and other information needed are available on the FBI's Web site (**www. fbi.gov**).

Other Documents and Items You Should Bring

If you are running from an abuser, bring any and all forms that document proof of the abuse. This includes photographs of injuries, videos of violent behavior, police reports, signed affidavits from witnesses of your abuse, or anything else that can offer proof you were in danger while living with this person. This will help you get the law on your side if the abuser does manage to find you.

Why You Should Not Fake Your Own Death

Faking one's death is illegal, and is known as pseudocide. This includes faking any suicide, accident, or murder. Pseudocide is not a good idea under any circumstances. If the fact that it is illegal is not enough to sway you, realize that the police are going to suspect you are still alive if there is no body. They will put more effort into finding you because they still have a chance of finding you alive. If your death involves an insurance claim — especially a large claim — you will have various trained investigators on your trail. They may not find you, but they are likely to uncover your ruse. Disappearing to manipulate insurance claims is fraud and you will be caught.

Besides the legal issues, all of the forensic tools that are now available make it nearly impossible to fool investigators. It is likely that your "disappearance" will not be believed.

An Englishman named Graham Cardwell, an assistant dock master in Lincolnshire, faked his own death in 1998. An extensive air and sea search was made after the discovery of a lifejacket and helmet belonging to Graham. Police found Graham eight months later under an assumed identity. Graham said he staged his death to prevent his family from learning he was dying of cancer. Despite the time and money spent searching for him, police declined to press charges. Police said an anonymous informant had found him. They would not say whom, but hinted that it was a family member living nearby as a bachelor who turned Graham in.

Again, it is *illegal* to fake your own death. This book is not advising that you take this action to begin a new life.

Clean Up for Before You Leave

As you get closer to departure, you need to start cleaning up your house. This does not mean vacuuming the floors, but collecting all your letters, bills, magazines, and receipts. Get a shredder from an office supply store and shred any evidence of you being there to ensure you do not leave behind identifying information that might connect you to your new life.

For maximum security, get a confetti-cut shredder that reduces your documents to thousands of tiny pieces. Burning a document also ensures it cannot be reconstructed. Whatever you do, do not send in change-of-address forms for magazines or anything that comes through the mail. It seems obvious, but it has led to the downfall of some individuals who took every other precaution.

If you know someone is going to come looking for you, take the time to find and destroy all recent photos of yourself. This may be impossible if you are a member of social networking site, where anyone can upload photos of you and save those photos to their computer. If you are able to destroy all recent photos of yourself, you eliminate an important resource people can use to locate you.

Do not assume that if the trash is set out in the front yard it will be picked up, and that is the end of it. If anyone wants to start looking for you, the trash is a treasure — assuming they get there before regular hours of pick up. Play it safe and dispose of your trash in multiple dumpsters far away from your home.

Revealing information that can be found in a person's trash includes:

- Statements or notices from your bank that list account numbers
- Statements or notices from credit companies that list account numbers or even your social security number
- Cell phone or landline telephone bills that provide detailed call lists
- Paycheck stubs from work that often include your social security number in part or whole
- Detailed receipts such as work order forms for your car
- Letters from friends or family members that contain personal information
- Insurance policies for yourself, your home, your car, and other belongings
- Tax documents, such as a W2
- Matchbooks – private investigators often check them because they may indicate a place where the person visits frequently and some people write phone numbers on them
- Itemized grocery and pharmacy slips
- Envelopes with foreign stamps can reveal your destination
- Classified ads from newspapers – private investigators look for where people sometimes circle addresses or other items

You do not need to keep most documents longer than three years. Even tax documents become dead weight after three years because the IRS can only dispute your return and audit you within three years of your file date, unless of course you intentionally lie on a return. Therefore, any documents you have to support old tax returns can be shredded, but it is still a good idea to keep a copy of your returns so you have an accurate picture of financial history.

Packing for Forever

While you should get rid of most of your possessions, there are other things you will want to make sure to take. Keep track of important documents and be sure to pack some basic supplies like a flashlight and batteries. One Bag (**www.onebag.com**) offers some great advice to those who want to travel light. Having a few small tools can be the difference between handling a minor emergency yourself and having to get help from others, which means more contact with people who can later identify you.

Other necessary items include:

- Passport
- Driver's license
- All identification cards
- Legal records
- Your will
- Financial documents
- Medical records
- Prescriptions
- Medications

You certainly want to travel as lightly as possible to make your disappearance as uncomplicated as you can, but you also need to consider the climate of the place where you are going. You should consider what clothing should be brought along as well as items you can discard. Research the local climate before packing.

It is also a wise idea, no matter how you are traveling, not to have expensive luggage that attracts attention. It also can attract a thief's eye. Old and battered suitcases are the best. Perhaps the most anonymous carrier of all is military-style duffel bags. They are cheap and long lasting, and no one pays them much attention.

If you cannot take everything you want with you, you have three choices:

- **Rent storage:** You can rent a storage building and leave your things there. These often operate in such a way that you pay for the first month's rent plus a small deposit. You will likely have to provide your name and contact information, as well as personal identification, when you first rent the storage space. Legally, you should use your real name, but be careful when giving out contact information. Some people may choose to provide fake contact information. You sign an agreement that if you fall behind in your payments, often a set time of three months, your landlord confiscates your possessions. As long as you remember to make your payments (using cash only), you can let your things stay in storage. You usually have to provide your own lock, so there is no real concern about anyone going through your left-behind belongings to look for clues.

- **Give it all away:** The Salvation Army, Goodwill Industries, and many other nonprofit social services agencies are happy to take your possessions and try to make use of them. Even automobiles can be given to charitable groups.

- **Sell your things:** Most of us have far more clothing than we ever will wear. Try this: Take a look around and leave anything behind that you have not used for three months. Put an ad in the newspaper, put up signs, and have a yard sale to get rid of belongings. Selling your items can also add to your cash reserves, which is very useful at this time.

chapter 3

Getting a New Identity

Anyone disappearing will want to create a new identity. To have a new identity, you need new identification. ID documents are necessary in order for you to travel and conduct financial transactions under your new name. These new documents will also throw others off your trail. Although you could try moving to another city and calling yourself by a new name, this is very risky because you are going to need a job, medical care, and a social network of friends. You will need proper identification to keep your old identity off of records that can lead to the police or a private investigator finding you.

Some people mistakenly think they can assume the identity of another person by using genuine identity cards. Say you found some credit cards and try to use these as identification. The person who lost those cards has a strong interest in getting them back. He or she notifies the police, and they are on your trail. This is identity theft, which is illegal and something you *should not even consider.* You cannot use another person's ID cards even if they are willing because you are still lying about your identity.

Changing Your Name

While changing your name is fairly easy and quite legal, the laws vary from state to state and most require a public announcement of some sort declaring your decision to change your name. Unfortunately, this is exactly what you are trying to avoid. If you need to get away quickly, you may want to move first and then obtain new IDs. In fact, some states, such as Michigan and Wyoming, require you to live there for a year or more before you can even apply for a name change. You can find out more about laws regarding changing your name at the NameChangeLaw.com Web site (**www.namechangelaw.com/states.htm**).

If you are changing your name to avoid being discovered by an abuser, most states will seal the records of your name change to the public. Law officers may still have access, but only if they are conducting a legal investigation. Because this procedure is common, you may actually be able to contact a lawyer or paralegal and ask what the laws are in your state or the state you are planning to move to. You will not likely need legal representation for a simple name change.

There are self-help legal Web sites for every state that can provide you with the information you need, such as this one for California: **www.courtinfo.ca.gov/selfhelp**. These sites are usually part of the state's official court Web site, which should also have the information you are looking for, but you may have to do some digging. Another Web site that has the information for every state is Nolo (**www.nolo.com**), but there are charges for various forms and booklets. If you still have trouble finding the information, call your county court and they should be able to help you.

There are four exceptions for changing your name:

1. You cannot change your name to flee financial obligations. This is called "fraudulent intent."

2. You cannot change your name to someone else's name and attempt to impersonate them. For example, you cannot go by Brad Pitt and then present yourself as the famous actor and try to get work. You will need to explain the reason behind your new name choice, and any moneymaking schemes will be denied.

3. You cannot change your name to include numbers or symbols, such as Bob(*)123. The only numbers you could potentially include would be roman numerals at the end to represent coming from a long lineage of those with the same name, such as Michael Charles IX, but as a person in hiding, you should avoid such a unique and outdated name.

4. You cannot have vulgar language in your name. Although there are adult movie stars who go by such names, these are just stage names and not legally changed names.

Believe it or not, you can unofficially change your name by consistently calling yourself by a new name. As long as you follow the same rules as the in-court name change procedure, such as not adding numbers or derogatory terms to your new name, or trying to hide from creditors or the police, you do not even have to go to court. Note that this will not legally change your name; you will need to go to court to have it changed at some point because most places will not accept your new name without legal documentation. It is still good to know that going by an assumed name is not illegal in any way.

Joining the French Foreign Legion

If you are male, you can also get a new identity by joining the French Foreign Legion, an elite military unit established in 1831. The legion was specifically created for foreign nationals wishing to serve in the French Armed Forces, but commanded by French officers. However, it is also open to French citizens, who amounted to 24 percent of the recruits as of 2007. The group consists of 7699 male Legionnaires; there has, officially, only ever been one female volunteer.

Open to people of any nationality, most Legionnaires still come from European countries, but a growing percentage comes from Latin America. While no serious studies have been made of the motives for enlistment, the majority of Legionnaires were once either transients in need of escape and a regular paycheck or refugees from countries undergoing crises. In recent years, however, the improved conditions and professionalism of the Legion have in turn attracted a new kind of recruit, from middle-class backgrounds in stable and prosperous countries, such as the United States, Britain, and France itself.

In the past, the Legion had a reputation for attracting criminals on the run and would-be mercenaries, but the admissions process is now severely restricted and background checks are performed on all applicants. Generally speaking, convicted felons are prohibited from joining the service. Legionnaires can choose to enlist under a pseudonym ("declared identity"). This disposition exists in order to allow people who want to start their lives over to enlist. French citizens can enlist under a declared, fictitious, foreign citizenship (often that of Canada or Monaco). After one year's service, Legionnaires can regularize their situation under their true identity. After serving in the Legion for three years, a legionnaire may apply for French citizenship. He must be serving under his real name, must no longer have problems with the authorities, and must have served with "honor and fidelity." Furthermore, a soldier who becomes injured during a battle for France can apply for French citizenship under a provision known as "Français par le sang versé" ("French by spilled blood").

You can learn more about the French Foreign Legion by visiting the group's recruiting Web site at **www.legion-recrute.com**.

Witness Security Program

The U.S. Marshals Service provides for the security, health, and safety of government witnesses and their immediate dependents, whose lives are in danger as a result of their testimony against drug traffickers, terrorists, organized crime members, and other major criminals.

The Witness Security Program was authorized by the Organized Crime Control Act of 1970 and amended by the Comprehensive Crime Control Act of 1984. The U.S. Marshals have protected, relocated, and given new identities to more than 8,200 witnesses and 9,800 of their family members, since the program began in 1971.

The successful operation of this program is widely recognized as providing a unique and valuable tool in the government's battle against major criminal conspirators and organized crime.

Witnesses and their families typically get new identities with authentic documentation. Housing, subsistence for basic living expenses, and medical care are provided to the witnesses. Job training and employment assistance may also be provided.

The U.S. Marshals provide 24-hour protection to all witnesses, while they are in a high-threat environment, including pretrial conferences, trial testimonials, and other court appearances.

No Witness Security Program participant who followed security guidelines has been harmed while under the active protection of the U.S. Marshals.

In both criminal and civil matters involving protected witnesses, the U.S. Marshals cooperate fully with local law enforcement and court authorities to bring witnesses to justice or to have them fulfill their legal responsibilities.

You can find out more information by visiting the U.S. Marshals' Web site (**www.usmarshals.gov**). You can also find additional information on how the process of becoming a protected witness works by visiting the HowStuffWorks Web site on the witness protection program (**http://people.howstuffworks.com/witness-protection.htm**).

Social Security Card

Social security numbers are another important part of your new IDs. It is not legal, of course, to change your social security number, unless you have permission from a judge and a court order. Individuals placed in witness protection programs sometimes get a new social security number, but other than that, it is virtually impossible to get a new one.

There are two categories of people who can get a new social security card number in addition those in the Witness Protection Program:

1. **Victims of identity theft that can prove their social security number was used to commit the theft.** The theft often has to be extensive and repeated; so one instance where someone tried to get a credit card using your SSN is not enough to get a new one.

2. **Victims of abuse from a spouse, family member, or dangerous stalker.** Each case is considered individually, so proof of abuse or harassment must also be supplied, mainly from third parties, such as police and physicians' records. You will need to apply in person at a social security office. The Social Security Administration recommends you change your name before applying for a new number so there is a clearer link between your old identity and your new one.

If you are hiding from an abuser, you can contact the Administration Domestic Violence Page (**www.ssa.gov/pubs/10093.html**), which offers new numbers to victims of domestic abuse by request. For other questions and information, go to the Social Security Administration's main site (**www.ssa.gov**) or call 1-800-772-1213.

If you for some reason do not have a social security card, or have lost yours, the Social Security Administration will need to see documents that prove your U.S. citizenship. These include a U.S. birth certificate, U.S. consular report of birth, or a passport. The Social Security Administration also accepts a limited array of documents to prove your identity. The documents cannot be expired and must supply your name and ideally a photograph. Common documents that prove identity include a U.S. driver's license, identification card, or U.S. passport. If you do not have these documents, substitute documents include:

- Employee ID card
- School ID card
- Marriage document
- Health insurance card (not a Medicare card)
- U.S. military ID card
- Adoption decree
- Life insurance policy

After you legally change your name, you will need to update your social security card. Your number will remain the same, but your new name must be associated with it so you can continue to file taxes and receive government benefits.

Driver's License

Driver's licenses are given out and regulated by each state, so the Unofficial DMV Guide (**www.dmv.org/changing-your-name.php**) provides the information for getting your new driver's license based on which state you are living in. It is not wise to take your old car, but if you choose to do so, you will likely have to change the title to reflect your new name.

International driving permit

If you plan to leave the United States and go to Europe, you should get an International Driving Permit. This card is provided by AAA and translates your driver's license information into ten European languages. If you plan on heading to South or Central America, you should get an Inter-American Driving Permit. The steps are the same for both cards and include filling out a form, supplying two passport-sized photographs (2x2 inches), a photocopy of the front and back of your driver's license, and a $15 fee. These driving permits will not serve as another form of ID in the United States, but are good to have as an American living — and driving — outside of the country. If you decide to permanently stay in another country, you will have to go through the process of becoming a legal citizen and then obtain a driver's license in that country. The International Driving Permit and Inter-American Driving Permit are only good for one year, and cannot be renewed. They also cannot be obtained any earlier than six months before your departure, and will take four to six weeks to arrive.

The Web site to obtain documents for the International Driving Permit is: **www.aaasouth.com/Travel/travel_drivers.aspx?nvbar=Travel:IntlDrivingPermit**.

The Web site to obtain documents for the Inter-American Driving Permit is: **www.aaasouth.com/documents/idp_app.pdf**.

Identification card

If you do not have a driver's license and would rather not get one, you can still get an identification card to verify your name and age. This card is obtained through the Department of Motor Vehicles, just like a driver's license, but usually just requires you to bring in your social security card and proof of residence. The individual state procedures can be found by visiting the Unofficial DMV Guide's Web site at **www.dmv.org/id-cards.php**.

Credit Cards

Whether or not you should continue using any credit cards you have or attempt to apply for a new credit card is up to you. No one can legally search for you based on your credit information unless they are government officials or the originating creditor. However, the police will likely be able to check your credit cards for charges to determine your location, and if anyone knows your social security number, former address, birth date, and your credit card number, they can submit a credit report at **AnnualCreditReport.com** (**www.annualcreditreport.com**).

Though this only provides a record of your payment, it also provides your contact information. Therefore, someone could potentially use your old address to find your new one. They can also see any requests you made against your credit, such as applying for new card. To prevent this, request your free copy and then put a security freeze on your account. It is a simple process you can enable with a few clicks after you retrieve your report.

In addition, moving away and starting a new life can be costly, and you are likely wondering how to obtain a credit card in your. Experts regarding voluntary disappearance often suggest the use of prepaid cards, such as one from NetSpend (**www.netspend.**

com), to minimize a paper trail. Think of them as a universal gift card you give yourself. This means use of a prepaid credit card will not be on your credit report, unless otherwise mentioned.

If you have good credit, think twice before cancelling your accounts. Although you want to disassociate yourself from your old life, closing an account that is in good standing can actually hurt your credit score. Instead of closing the account, call the credit card company and explain that you will not be using your account for an extended period of time and ask what you should do to secure the account without having to close it. They will be more than happy to assist you. Do not reveal too much information though, and keep your request simple if they ask why you will not be using your card. Make up a believable claim, like you are traveling out of the country and will not be taking your card with you. Credit card representatives can be extremely pushy and nosy due to the nature of their job (getting people to pay their balance), so just remember you do not have to answer their personal questions because you are not doing anything wrong.

If you are looking to leave the country and become an expatriate (a person who temporarily or permanently resides in a country and culture other than that of the person's upbringing or legal residence), you should know that your credit history does not follow you if you get a credit card in a new country. This can be good news or bad news depending on your credit worthiness, and may affect your decision to move outside the United States.

Passport

If you are planning to leave the United States, you will need a passport. This process takes four to six weeks, but there is an option for expedited service that may reduce the time to two to three weeks. However, it costs an additional $60 plus overnight shipping costs and does not guarantee you will actually get your passport in that amount of time. The only way to get your passport sooner is to make an appointment at a regional passport agency, but there are only 17 of these offices in the United States, so you may be hundreds of miles away from the nearest one.

If you already have a valid passport but need to update your name after changing it, there are three categories, and each has slightly different procedures:

1. You have had your passport less than a year and need to change your name.
2. You have had it more than a year and need to change your name.
3. You cannot legally show your name change with a marriage license or court order.

The last option is only for people who have used an assumed name for over five years and have three public records that prove their identity. All three options require you to mail in your current passport, completed form, two 2x2 color photographs of your face, and accepted proof of your name change.

You also need to check the laws of the country you are traveling to, as some require your passport to be valid for at least six months after your entrance into the country, and you may also need to have a certain number of blank stamp pages to be allowed in. The Department of State has a special section on their Web site (**www.travel.state.gov**) called "Country Specific Information" which is located on the left toolbar. Here you will find the laws for travel to every country in the world, so research the country you wish to go to and make sure it is really the best choice for you, especially if you are going to attempt to become a citizen.

If you have children who are under the age of 16, you cannot get them a passport without the consent of the other parent. This involves both parents and the child going to a Passport Acceptance Facility, like a post office and providing proof of citizenship and identification. This is to prevent one parent from kidnapping a child and then fleeing the country.

For more information, visit: the Department of State's Web site at **http://travel.state.gov/passport/passport_1738.html**.

Can you have more than one passport?

The answer is yes, people can have more than one passport. However, there are many ways of getting a second passport, and the laws vary worldwide. A U.S. passport will allow access into almost every country, so unless you plan to become a citizen of that country, you should not need another passport. You cannot legally have two U.S. passports that are not identical for national security reasons, but there are cases in which you can have a duplicate passport, such as if you must send your passport off to get a visa but also need to travel during that time. Therefore, if you want to leave the country under a new name, you have to legally change your name and then apply for a new passport. If you are interested in a duplicate U.S. passport, call the National Passport Information Center at 1-877-487-2778 to find out the procedures.

Some countries welcome individuals with nationalized ancestors. Others give passports to certain religious groups. Some passports can be obtained simply by buying real estate. The variations are endless, but the quickest, easiest way to get a second passport is to buy it. There are two main ways of getting a second passport. You can go to a service or through the government.

There are many other advantages to having a second passport. If it is from another country, you will have more freedom to travel around the world, as you never know when diplomatic situations may change between countries. You could find yourself essentially trapped in a country should they change the laws for "security purposes."

Countries that claim to have created provisions for not singling out wealthy individuals are often not presenting a complete picture. Canada, Australia, and New Zealand are among countries that are particularly eager to attract wealthy residents. The Philippines is another example of a country known for allowing wealthy individuals to obtain passports, often on condition that they do not compete with the native workforce.

Buying real estate to get a passport

There are citizenship-by-investment programs in certain countries that exist to draw funds by offering remarkable deals to investors. Probably the most well know is St. Kitts and Nevis program, where an investor can either purchase government-approved properties that include condominiums or villas (raw land does not qualify in the program) or make a donation of $200,000. If you plan to live there, the housing option makes more sense. The motivation for the government is to encourage the development of residential and tourism projects. The minimal amount of $350,000 has at times been changed, but their program is costly because there are other fees. In addition to purchasing the property, there is a one-time fee of $35,000.

Other incidental costs are also involved, such as transfer fees. That amount of $350,000 ends up being closer to $420,000. On a positive note, there are no restrictions on how long you must hold a property. In reality, you could buy the property on a Monday and sell it the following Tuesday. Another complication is that you can only sell to another person involved in the program. However, once you are citizen you do not have to pay any income taxes, or taxes on inheritances or gifts. You also do not have to renounce your U.S. citizenship as St. Kitts and Nevis recognize dual citizenship.

Two other countries that offer special economic citizenship programs are Belize and Grenada. With an investment of $50,000 you can get a passport almost immediately.

Another way to qualify for a second passport is through marriage, family ties, or a residence for a lengthy period of time. St.

Kitts and Nevis is among areas that make it incredibly simple to get a passport. Depending on your financial conditions, you should hire a lawyer to explore your options. There are many firms that specialize in the field of second passports.

For more information, visit the Offshore Advisor Web site at **www.isla-offshore.com/services/citizenship-st-kitts-nevis**. Download the PDF entitled "Citizenship-by-Investment in the Federation of St. Kitts and Nevis."

Find a lawyer to help in your passport search

A lawyer can help in finding other countries where the government hands out passports and citizenship in return for a monetary investment. There are often high sums, up to $350,000 or more, to give to government-approved real estate projects, sometimes called economic citizenship programs. The real estate you buy is likely not going to be a bargain, and you often have to pay in cash to qualify.

There are also stipulations of participation for a number of years. Most of the jurisdictions offering these programs do not require the investing individual to live there, but they often stipulate that you travel in and out occasionally. Not all of these programs come with a second passport, and they change from time to time. That is why you will almost certainly need to contact a lawyer specializing in this field to narrow down your search of where to obtain a second passport.

You should also look into the ramifications of having a second passport, and ask yourself and your lawyer questions, including the following:

- Are there tax advantages in getting a passport from one country or another?
- Does this country have an income tax?
- What about other taxes?
- Is this a place where I might want to live?
- Is political and or economic stability an issue?
- How much am I willing to pay, or how much money can I invest?

Another issue is how to sort out what kind of second passport you want. Here are a few elements that define a good second passport:

- It should be suitable for asset protection and banking.
- The country originating it should have a low profile.
- It should be from a reliable, trusted, and true program.

Second passport mistakes

Furthermore, some companies say they will file for a name change and get you a second passport in a new name. That sounds like a good idea, but you want to be careful because changing your name at the same time you get a second passport can lead to trouble. The reason is that many countries since Sept. 11 get listings of all name changes filed in all countries. The government is up on these things. You might call attention to yourself and even start to show up in various databases. It is better to use only the name you have now for your passports, assuming that you have already changed it. People traveling with different passports in different names arouse immediate suspicions. All your carried documents should be in the same name.

Some companies also offer diplomatic passports, but this is not a good idea for you. It is virtually impossible to legally get that kind of document.

Alternative passport options

If you cannot afford several thousand dollars for a second passport, do not worry. There are several countries where you can easily establish a residency leading to a passport. Often, these countries give you a temporary residency pass and allow you to get a new passport within two to three years. These are not economic citizenship passports, but they often allow you to travel visa-free to more than 100 nations.

Currently, there is also something called the Panama Instant Passport Program, but you will need to check because the program availability changes. It is essentially free. You place $175,000 into the Panama National Bank locked into a five-year Certificate of Deposit paying you $750 in interest monthly. Panama then issues a five-year passport. This passport is good for travel throughout Central and South America and some Western European countries.

The passport also qualifies you for a Panama driver's license. This program can often be completed in a few weeks. The advantage is that you have a second passport and a driver's license — essentially a whole set of identification references. After getting this passport, you can choose another country in Central and South America and establish residency. Your residency there will allow you to get a passport from still another country, which is handy because your Panama passport expires after five years.

Fake IDs

You may have encountered businesses or individuals who will create fake identification or "novelty" identification cards. There are many sites, but those who have tried them out have either gotten nothing after mailing their money or found that the identification card was worthless and unusable. Some sites claim they have foolproof secrets to generating fake identification cards, but again this is a lie to make money.

Being caught with a fake identification card is generally a misdemeanor. Penalties vary but can include jail time. In some states, the act of using a fake identification card is a felony. This book does not advocate the use of any fake identification cards.

100000
60000
40000
20000
0
Balance
Assets
60000
40000
20000

chapter 4

Deciding Where to Go

Sometime during the early stages of planning your disappearance, you should start thinking about where to go. The first decision will be whether to stay in the United States or live overseas as an expatriate – someone who lives in a country other than his or her place of citizenship. Whatever your decision, your new location should be outside of your present city and state. If you happened to tell friends you always wanted to live in San Francisco, do not make that your choice. Someone may recall that, which makes locating you much simpler.

Also, think about your specific needs when you look at possible locations. Are you thinking of gaining citizenship in another country? What if you have to renounce your U. S. citizenship – is this something you would consider? What if you fall in love and want to marry someone in another country? Is that going to affect your citizenship? Something else to look at carefully is your own lifestyle and comfort level. Many native-born Americans do not adjust well to living in a country where they are in a minority and do not have the rights they are accustomed to as an American citizen.

People sometimes think that distance creates safety, so they choose to live thousands of miles away. In many ways, it is easier to escape detection when you leave the United States far behind, but the move can create other problems and issues. If you do decide to leave for a distant location, this book will provide the answers you need to accomplish this goal.

Staying in the United States

One problem with staying in the United States with another identity is that it has been done so often. Many people have tried it before you and have created a blueprint that both government and private investigators can follow to check your personal, business, and financial activities. It is also much easier for anyone who is looking for you to only have to deal with other Americans. This cuts out expensive international calls, possible overseas trips, and possible language barriers for those searching for you.

When considering whether to stay in the United States or to move to another country, keep in mind that the best searches require financial resources. People who send out investigators to locate someone often have limited budgets. Debt collectors, for example, might not want to spend more money after they have already lost thousands of dollars. On the other hand, dedicated searchers with more time and money are a serious threat. Therefore, the primary concern is to carefully cover your tracks to make it so time-consuming and expensive to find you that no one wants to start the search.

There are also many reasons to stay in the United States. You are familiar with the culture and most people speak your language. You know your way around and have likely been to other areas of the country, so you have ways of comparing lifestyles in different regions. If you know you want to stay in the United States, you will need to decide where you want to live.

A major problem to consider is that the United States is the most computerized country in the world. Computers are adding more material daily that cross-references everyone's personal business and financial transactions. It all starts with social security and ends in death insurance claims. Every move you make in the United States is reported and analyzed. Much of that information is sold to anyone who can pay the price.

There is certainly more information available about you if you live in the United States than if you decide to leave and head to another country. These government agencies maintain extensive databases, but they are commonly not motivated to act on what they know, unless someone is making a gargantuan effort to locate you. These agencies also tend to move slowly.

Obviously, unless you want to stay on the move constantly, you need some kind of address. Homeless people cannot start bank accounts or send out checks to pay their bills. So you need to find a temporary place to start, and then move on to some kind of permanent residence – unless you want to travel constantly, which is the preference of some who vanish, particularly if they have a source of income without having to work.

You might want to start out by staying in a hotel. This is about as anonymous as you can get. This has become far more feasible in recent years, as extended-stay places have popped up everywhere, offering all the conveniences of your own home. Hotels do not require credit backgrounds. The hotels supply most of essential services, such as electricity, freeing you from having to fill out applications for local utility companies. Some extended-stay properties are as inexpensive as $200 to $300 a week and come with kitchens. In theory, you could stay for as long as you wanted. Take into account, however, that many states have added stiff taxes that long-stay hotels often do not advertise.

You could also check the daily newspapers and the Internet for ads for a "room to share," "rentals to share," or "apartments to share." All records in these cases should be in someone else's name. You should try to make arrangements with the already-existing tenant to be kept out of the lease or any other records. This arrangement is particularly good for someone trying to put some distance between an old identity and a new one. When your new identify is totally set up, you can be confident that you have vanished in the interim period.

Do not get too friendly with your roommate. If you hold up your end of the bargain by paying rent and whatever else is required you will likely be left alone. Remember that landlords are excellent sources of information for anyone who comes looking for you, so if you want to get personal with your roommate, tell misleading stories about where you grew up, places you want to visit, and where your family members are for the purpose of throwing off anyone who is looking for clues to find you.

You might try telling him or her that you are thinking of returning to college or going "back east." It may be tempting not to pay your final rent because, after all, you are leaving, but do not succumb to that idea. It will make your roommate an enemy who will be happy to cooperate with anyone looking for you if the opportunity comes up. J. Edgar Hoover said 90 percent of all arrests by the FBI were due directly to the helpful cooperation of neighbors and friends.

For most people, there are everyday practicalities to consider. You will eventually want to find a place to settle down. Most people also need a job, a roof over their heads, and a permanent place to stay.

Rule Out Best Places to Live

In 2010, *Money Magazine* came up with the best places to live in the United States, based on school ratings, home prices, crime rates, and much more. The top ten were:

- Eden Prairie, MN
- Columbia/Ellicott City, MD
- Newton, MA
- Bellevue, WA
- McKinney, TX
- Fort Collins, CO
- Overland Park, KS

- Fishers, IN
- Ames, IA
- Rogers, AR
- Plymouth, MN

If choosing to disappear, you do not want to live in any of these places. They are simply too small and friendly for you. *Money Magazine* said its list, "focused on smaller places that offered the best combination of economic opportunity, good schools, safe streets, things to do, and a real sense of community." A "sense of community" is something you want to avoid. It translates into a small group of people who know too much about everyone else. That does not mean you have to live in a big city to be anonymous, but there are at least three compelling reasons to live in a larger city:

1. You blend in easier. Anyone looking for you will simply have to search harder. Plus, if someone is only casually attempting to find you, the search may be difficult enough to discourage him or her.

2. In a small town, many want, and expect, to know everything about any new residents, which makes it easier to have a slip of the tongue that may give you away when you are casually chatting with a friendly neighbor.

3. If you need to find work to support yourself, there are many more job opportunities in larger cities.

Once you are settled in your new area, you most likely will want to stay there a while. If you happen to be in an employment field that begins to decline, and you lose your job, you want to be able to find something in your adopted hometown. That is obviously much easier when there are larger numbers of people and more job opportunities.

If you need to work, you will have to relocate to areas where there are jobs in your particular field. Of course, American cities are undergoing many changes. Those in the automotive field in the past might have named Detroit as an attractive city for relocation, but the industry has been in a steady decline.

When looking at other factors outside of employment, the best place for you is an area where many people are coming and going so you do not stand out. Central Florida, for example, is a transient area where most people are newcomers. It also has a varied employment base that has expanded well beyond tourism into medical, educational, and technical fields.

Ultimately, where you decide to live is your choice. Here are some guidelines that may help narrow your search:

- You want to live in a medium or large town where you will face less scrutiny and not be around a lot of particularly "friendly" people.

- Unless you are independently wealthy, you want to live somewhere that offers you job opportunities in your particular profession.

- You should pick somewhere you fit in and do not stand out as an obvious "outsider" who attracts attention and, worse, curiosity. If you are a southerner with a deep drawl, you would be seen as extremely out of place in Vermont or

Maine, which could raise suspicions. If anyone ever came looking for you, you would be easier to find because you were known as the "southerner."

- You do not want to move to an area that seems to have a lot of intolerance or bias toward newcomers.
- In the event that you have a concentration of relatives or acquaintances in some city or another, it is a good idea to leave that area off your most-desirable list.

Big American Cities are Better

In regard to large American cities, there is some benefit to getting lost in the crowd. Some American cities are quickly characterized and can be encapsulated in just a few words or images. New York City, for example, is the United States' largest and has vast diversity. It is the Big Apple, and it is a 24-hour city with museums, nightlife, many restaurants, and a high quality of life. It is an expensive city with a high cost of living.

San Francisco is another quality American city, and the Bay area is considered a good place to live. Los Angeles is another city where it is easy to lose yourself, but it is also spread out and you have to drive everywhere, which is daunting for some people. Chicago is wonderful city with much to offer, but it is extremely cold in the winter.

Obviously, you have to go beyond these generalizations and conduct some research into areas of the United States that are of interest to you. Useful resources include local chambers of commerce, libraries, bookstores, and the Internet.

With a few exceptions, areas that are attractive to you can be looked at under the same criteria that you would use if you were not a "missing" person. For example, in addition to the key element of job availability, here is a ten-point list for judging the desirability of one city or another:

1. Compare your new home with where you live now. Chances are, you want something similar, so compare it in terms of livability.
2. Be aware of the climate. If you cannot stand cold weather, you should look favorably at the Sun Belt states.
3. Evaluate the cost of living. If it is high, such as it is in New York City, put it on the minus side.
4. If you like outdoor activities and nature, consider what is offered in various cities.
5. Examine how the area measures up in regard to housing, transportation, and congestion.
6. Determine whether the area has special interest for you in terms of its aesthetics, such as old buildings and interesting stores.
7. Explore the art and culture. If this is of any interest to you at all, you should take a good look at what is available.
8. Narrow your findings down to a short list. Sites such as Sperling's BestPlaces (**www.bestplaces.net**), which lists the pluses and minuses of hundreds of cities, will help.

9. Do your homework. Look at statistics. Read the local newspapers. Make personal visits.

10. Make a chart of the pluses and minuses from all the information you have gathered. Keep in mind that no place is perfect, and you are not going to make a decision based just on numbers, but this should help guide you in making this important decision.

If you are like most Americans, you will likely look first at the areas of largest growth in the United States. They are in the West, the Sunbelt, and along the I-95 corridor between Raleigh, North Carolina and Atlanta, Georgia. In a sense, Americans who relocate without thoughts of disappearing follow the sun.

Another fast-growing area to consider is Clark County, Nevada, which includes the city of Las Vegas, because of its tremendous growth and its proportion of newcomers. Some residents have said that the common mood in the desert hub of "good weather, gambling, tourism, and an easy lifestyle" creates an area where strangers are welcomed without any questions asked.

If you are having trouble deciding where to go, or are indecisive about the whole question, there are various Web sites you can turn to for help. One of the best is Sperling's BestPlaces (**www.bestplaces.net**). The site, started in 1985, offers a software program that allows users to enter their personal preferences to help guide them to their own best places. The guide allows users to give a number for the importance of such factors as climate, crime, arts and culture, and regulations of various areas of the country. Users add up their scores when completing the exercise, which gives them some indication of where they might be most satisfied.

Buying a Home

Your identity documents play a part in selecting your new home. For example, if you do not yet have a driver's license, it will be impossible to buy a home through regular channels of real estate acquisition.

When you buy a home through the usual resources, there are always lawyers and real estate agents involved. They will be asking you for various forms of identification, but the only time you will absolutely have to provide these documents is at a closing. Therefore, you should be prepared at that time to have valid documents that will pass a cursory check. The best, most useful form of identity is your driver's license, and then perhaps a credit card or two.

Anonymous buyers in most states can receive a title to real property without signing any forms. If you do not require a mortgage, you do not have to sign anything. The first element for you to avoid as a buyer is a realtor. Avoid retaining the services of a buyer's agent. Do not respond to ads that list properties through real estate agents. You want to find a home being sold by the owner.

If you choose to rent an apartment instead of a home, you will find it is difficult to stay invisible. One major reason is that apartment managers have had plenty of experience with unreliable renters, so they are generally determined to know who you are to be sure you will be paying them regularly.

In the wake of Sept. 11, rental landlords may require all the items below:

- Your driver's license and a second piece of identification, such as a credit card
- The name, address, and telephone number of one or more references, possibly relatives
- Your social security number, which will allow the landlord to check databases of undesirable tenants
- The name of your employer, proof of your monthly income, and perhaps a paycheck stub
- If self-employed, a copy of your most recent tax return
- Your date of birth
- The name of your bank and even your account number or a bank statement
- A signed contract that includes a list of your most recent landlords with their telephone numbers
- Typically, at least one reference

Not every one of these items is always required, but you should be ready to provide at least some of them. To possibly get around these daunting requirements, you might dress well and offer to pay several months in advance. Also, stay away from large, corporate apartments and opt for landlord-owners, who might be far more willing to take you at face value without much background checking. The larger corporations often have policies that make it difficult for you to maintain your anonymity.

If you see no way to get around these requirements, do not worry. Get a short lease or rent month-by-month while you search for a more permanent place.

Consider sub-renting. Check out newspapers, Internet sites, and bulletin boards for ads under "rooms to share" or "apartments to share." If you choose this route, all records related to occupancy will already be in someone else's name. You can make arrangements to pay in cash with the current occupant. Even the landlord may not know who you are. This is an excellent way to maintain anonymity.

If you choose to rent a house from a private individual, you will likely be subject to a less stringent background check. The object here is to deal directly with the owner of the property. He or she will likely be happy if you claim privacy as a reason for not having more identification. Additionally, offer to pay for six months' rent on a six-month lease, or a year if you can afford it.

An alternative to a home or apartment is a travel trailer or mobile home. These are generally low-priced and often overlooked as sources for housing. You might look at used, older mobile homes that may be priced low enough so paying cash does not raise suspicions.

If you choose to buy a home, you will, in all probability, not be paying cash, though that is the least traceable way to do it. Instead, you might consider paying all your bills by forming a limited liability company. This can be complicated, and you may want to consult a lawyer, but at its simplest, you are forming a partnership without the need for a partner. Like a corporation, this is a legal entity that stands alone, but it lacks the many bookkeeping details and annual meetings required of a corporation. It has many advantages for someone trying to keep their name from appearing in public documents.

Only the owners of limited liability companies know the identity of the owner(s). The designation does not require an Internal Revenue Service (IRS) identification number or the keeping of books. Each state has its own form for forming a limited liability company. These are available online, usually for a nominal charge or $25 or so. The forms require you to name your company, select a profession, supply a mailing address, the names of any other partners, and other information. Forms are fairly simple, but keep in mind that they vary by state. Some states, such as New Mexico, allow you more privacy and require less details of your new company than others.

Anonymity through trusts

Another way to buy real estate is through a trust. These are often confusing and intimidating to people because they fulfill a variety of different purposes, ranging from living, land, and business trusts. Some of them are mainly for estate planning, but the business trust can be extremely useful to vanishing individuals because the trustee (attorney, bank, law firm) are the titleholders while the individual is the beneficiary. The individual still maintains control of the trust because the trustee cannot act without permission.

Some states make it legal to place real estate assets in a trust with undisclosed beneficiaries. In some states, you do not even need to file the paper with the registrar of deeds, which is the optimum situation for keeping your anonymity. If your particular state does not permit land trusts, you can get around that by setting up a standard business trust where you will place personal property.

If you are unable to pay cash to help keep your identity as secret as possible, there are alternatives. Consider buying undeveloped acreage, particularly in rural areas. Absentee owners often own these properties and may use them for hunting or occasional getaways. Many owners are anxious to sell, and they often are not interested in the buyer's background. They also may be receptive to creative financing.

Developer financing is another possibility. Your driver's license is often enough identification to satisfy a developer selling improved land. Developers will find the land, subdivide it, survey it, conduct site and water tests, and get the land ready for buyers. All you have to do is find a way to finance it. Lots sold this way often only require 10 percent down payments.

Some developers will require that credit forms be filled out. Owners often do not bother to check these forms, but even if they did and there was no file for you, it would most likely not derail the deal. Most of the time, developers feel protected by caveats in the mortgage agreement that say they can foreclose if bills are not paid within 30 days. These kinds of closings can often be done by mail, which happens even more frequently when you are dealing with an out-of-state seller.

After you have acquired raw land, you can simply hire someone to build a house. If you are on a budget, it is not unheard of to buy a pop-up trailer and live there for a while. If you have some carpentry skills or the ability to learn, you might build a house mostly by yourself. You need some expertise for items such as electrical wiring, but you can contract these out to private individuals. You will have to get building permits, which can be traced, but anyone looking for you will likely not even think of that avenue for unlocking your secret life. If you hire someone to do your work, he or she might be the "upfront," or person of record, as well.

Some of this chapter applies even if you have left the United States, but maintaining your anonymity overseas is more complicated.

Leaving the United States

Deciding to leave your homeland, especially for a country where you may spend the rest of your life, is not an easy decision. One way to make it easier is to do your homework. First, you need to honestly decide if you could handle moving out of the country by yourself and setting up a new life. If you think you can, then you need to research as many countries as possible to find one that suits your needs.

Various surveys have found that most people who immigrate to other countries later say they had no idea what the experience would be like. To decide whether you are a good candidate to move out of the United States, you might want to answer a few questions, such as:

1. How do you manage on your own? When you first move abroad, you will leave your support network of family, friends, and work colleagues behind. This is true wherever you disappear, but even more so in the case of expatriates.

2. How do you feel about travel? Those who move abroad are usually eager to travel about and see the surrounding area and nearby countries. Pause here a minute: If you hate the thought of further travel, are you sure you want to live abroad? Think about this before you decide to move.

3. Are you mentally and physically fit? Moving is quite an upheaval, and moving abroad is mentally and physically draining. You need to be in the right frame of mind and in good health to cope with the move. Health-care services overseas may not be available to you as soon as you arrive.

4. Are you capable and resourceful? What if your car broke down in a foreign country where you do not speak the language and you have no phone number for a mechanic? How would you manage in a new house if the electric or water go off and you have no one to ask about getting them reconnected? Would you break down, or would you roll your sleeves up and get on with it? Consider these questions before you move to a different country.

5. Are you skilled at learning new languages? Can you learn a new language quickly, or do you struggle with anything other than English? Learning the language is an important aspect to living in a new country.

6. Are you adventuresome? Despite the hard challenges of moving, of course, you will be transplanted into new and sometimes unsettling circumstances amidst strangers. How well do you adapt to change? These are important characteristics to consider when thinking of moving to a different country.

Still feeling comfortable about moving out of the country? Good, now you can start researching various countries, asking these questions as you go:

- Are there cultural, religious or language barriers?
- Could I easily obtain citizenship as a permanent resident?
- Could I find a job there?
- How does the health-care system compare with the American system?
- How efficient is the country's transportation network?
- Is the country a democracy, dictatorship, or anarchy?
- Would I find the political climate favorable, or frightening?
- What is the status of human rights in the country?
- Are there many other American expatriates who live in the country?
- Would the climate be agreeable?

This book cannot provide you with all the information you need to make a decision on where to relocate. The research is up to you. It is suggested that you make a list of pros and cons of the various areas as you conduct research.

Research could include visiting the Web sites of countries you are interested in, which provide information ranging from immigration to employment opportunities. You can also contact the United States Embassy to speak with someone about emigrating and what it entails. Another valuable resource for information about living abroad is the U.S. Department of State's Web site **http://travel.state.gov/travel/living/living_1243.html**.

It is far easier to emigrate if you have a job, but that is most likely not the case. The policy of different countries varies widely. In Canada, for example, immigration decisions are based on a point system, such as work experience and language proficiency. There, you are given a number of points if you already have a job or have been offered a position before arriving. In Australia, you can qualify for permanent visa status if you are a "skilled worker." In South Africa, skilled workers, such as industrialists or entrepreneurs, are in high demand and are most likely to be granted immigration status.

There are certain countries you can immediately rule out unless you have a special affinity or there are some compelling reasons you want to live there. Africa, for example, is commonly regarded as dangerous and undesirable. The climate is quite humid and corruption is rife, such as the modern-day pirates off the Horn of Africa. The Middle East has become somewhat more stable in recent years, but Israel is subject to ongoing acts of terrorism. Most people live in a state where carrying a gun is commonplace. There are checkpoints where police will possibly be taking a close look at your papers, so this is not a good place for someone looking to live a quiet life anonymously.

Tips for Americans Living Abroad

According to the U.S. Department of State, if you are planning to live abroad, you should take advantage of the agency's "register with embassies" program. Registering at the U.S. Embassy or Consulate in the country you are living in makes your whereabouts known in the event of an emergency. During any kind of emergency, American consular officers will be able to reach you as long as they know where you are.

The department recommends these elementary steps to you if you plan to live abroad:

- Assemble all vital documents, such as passports, birth and marriage records, vaccination records, insurance information, and bank records, in one readily accessible location.

- Check to be sure your passport and any necessary visas are valid and that you are registered at the Embassy/Consulate with your current address and phone number. If you need to obtain a new passport or update your registration, do so at the Embassy as soon as possible.

- Visa processing can take several weeks. Immediate family members should keep their U.S. visas current and apply for visas with as much time in advance of planned travel as possible.

- Make or update as necessary a complete inventory of your household effects, in duplicate.

- Maintain an adequate supply of food, water, and necessary medications in your home. Make sure your car is in good working order. Keep the gas tank full and check oil, coolant, tires, and battery frequently.

When a crisis occurs abroad, such as a natural disaster, transportation accident, civil or political unrest, or a terrorist incident, the Department of State and the U.S. Embassy abroad utilize a variety of means to communicate with the American public.

If you are in a foreign country involved in a crisis:

- Monitor the Department of State Web site, Bureau of Consular Affairs Web site, and the Web site for the U.S. Embassy in the foreign country for up-to-date information about the crisis.
- If a crisis occurs in a country you are visiting, contact your family in the United States to reassure them of your whereabouts and safety.
- Contact the U.S. Embassy or Consulate if you need help.
- Be sure to register with the U.S. Embassy or Consulate online, by phone, e-mail, fax, or in person. Registration helps consular staff contact you if necessary and allows you to receive situation updates.
- Monitor Voice of America and BBC broadcasts for announcements.

Before you decide to leave the United States, visit the U.S. Department of State's Web site (**http://travel.state.gov**) to find more information on the country in which you choose to live.

The Four Most Popular Expat Countries

Most Americans who decide to live in another country as "expats" select one of four destinations: Canada, Mexico, the United Kingdom, or Australia. In some surveys, including one completed by the Economist Intelligence Unit, both Australia and Canada fared well as desirable countries for relocation. Melbourne and Vancouver were cited as the best cities in the world for expatriates.

The survey gave 130 cities a "hardship" rating that looked at various criteria, including climate, cultural and recreational activities, and other factors. The cities with the lowest scores were designated the best places. Melbourne and Vancouver only had a 1 percent hardship mark. Vancouver would have earned a zero except for its climate, which includes four seasons.

Expatriates should avoid cities with marks of 20 or greater, the survey said. Cities with marks of 65 or greater are not even worth visiting. All Canadian cities that were reviewed received high marks. Toronto and Calvary earned a five. By comparison, most cities in the United States were between ten and 20. The best in America was Honolulu, at 7 percent, and the worst was Washington, D.C., at 19.

Canada

If you want a Western country, but do not want to go too far away, consider relocating to Canada. If for some reason you need to be close to the United States for business or other purposes, Canada is right across the border. Nova Scotia is a popular province. Nova Scotia has historic small towns, an idyllic countryside,

3,600 miles of rugged coastline punctuated with fishing villages, and a variety of outdoor recreation.

Partly because of the strengthening Canadian dollar, the country has drawn favorable reviews by Americans. A recent poll found that 92 percent of Americans had a favorable view of Canada. In addition, the number of Americans immigrating to Canada is at its highest point in 30 years. This is a major advantage because it makes it easier for someone seeking invisibility to get lost in the crowd. Canada also has generous government benefits. It remains relatively easy to emigrate there, as so many young Americans found out when they wanted to duck the Vietnam War. Perhaps its only drawback is the cold winters.

Security has tightened since Sept. 11, but it is still not difficult to relocate there if you have a job or are highly qualified in a desirable field. There are five general visa types for immigrants to Canada. The "skilled worker" and "professional class" visas are the most popular because it allows people to earn a living in Canada without being a citizen.

It would help if you have one of the skills in demand, such as working in the oil fields. You can find out more about what jobs and skills are most wanted on the Canadian Immigration Web site (**www.cic.gc.ca**). You should also be aware that Canada has a point system for accepting new immigrants, and the job situation is a major factor. There is a test on the immigration Web site that evaluates whether you are eligible to immigrate to Canada and what visa to apply for. For example, fluency in French will help immensely if applying to a French-speaking province. Some Canadian provinces issue special visas under the category "provincial nominees." Once you get to Canada by this method, you can always leave.

If you are seriously considering Canada, why not visit there on holiday and apply for a work permit? Visas are usually granted faster to those who already have a job lined up in Canada. When you visit, you should interview potential employers and let them know you would like to relocate, without telling them you want to disappear.

You will probably be welcomed with open arms if you have backing or capital and want to start a business in Canada, employ people, and generate taxable revenue. Investors, entrepreneurs, and self-employed people can apply for visas under a different section of the code. Another form of citizenship is family sponsorship.

Please remember that it is illegal to lie to any government official about your identity, such as when you are applying for a visa. It is suggested that you speak with an immigration attorney if you have any questions on this matter.

Mexico

A warm climate and affordable lifestyle are the primary reasons why an estimated 400,000 Americans and Canadians live in Mexico on a long-term basis. The largest community is in Lake Chapala, with a total of 40,000 expatriates. Mexico is close to the United States, so it is cheaper and easier to reach than a transoceanic country. But, like all places, there are drawbacks.

CASE STUDY: THE PLAIN TRUTH ABOUT LIVING IN MEXICO

Douglas Brewer

My wife and I are now beginning our fourth year as American expats in Guanajuato, Mexico. Sometimes it seems only yesterday that we sold all we owned in Overland Park, Kan., and moved here with just suitcases, nothing more. Sometimes it seems like we never had a beginning, but have always lived here.

I think, however, no matter how long we stay, we will always be foreigners. No matter how many of the locals we know, how many dinners and parties we are invited to, we will always be strangers. We will always be the American gringos, a slang word for American foreigners, from the Midwest.

I came to Mexico with no expectations. I intellectually knew and understood that Mexicans, though wonderfully lovely people, are just as fallible as I am. And, they most certainly are. I did not come expecting paradise. I knew I would find bugaboos and problems. Mexico and her people do not have a utopia south of the American Border.

But, I must admit, I was hoping that culturally there would be some sort of respite in Mexico from what had originally driven my wife and I from America. There had to be something, somewhere that could provide relief from the American cultural meltdown that so repulsed us. There just had to be.

There was.

Mexico did indeed provide a surprise that still, to this day, charms us. When we did our fact-finding trip to Guanajuato to see if this was the place for us, what we immediately noticed was *the absence of public rage*. We did not find what is so common in America whose citizens think it is socially appropriate behavior to "cut loose" whenever the spirit moves them, showing just how violent and mean they can be.

Another relief soothing to the heart is to see how family is not fractured here. Family, right down to cousins fourth and fifth removed, are part of the well-being of this society. Some of them live in family compounds, generations of them, and do so in peace, harmony, love and respect. I envy this greatly.

For the most part, we have been treated with the greatest degree of respect. Some have made us feel like we are their long-lost American cousins who have finally come home to where we belong. We have been invited into their homes (no small privilege if you know Mexican culture) and sometimes into their lives.

Mexicans, almost without exception, treat Americans with respect. They show far more respect than we Americans deserve considering how we have historically treated Mexicans and still do to this day. There are some, however, that have a passive-aggressive relationship with the American expat community. Where this comes from is anyone's guess. But, there are little, subtle, and almost unnoticeable things that you usually do not see as a tourist. You have to live here and carefully observe behavior to see that are a few snakes in paradise.

One day, while walking home on one of Guanajuato's rather narrow sidewalks, a Mexican woman stopped us and politely lectured us. She said because we were Americans, we should walk on the *outside* part of the sidewalk, nearest the street, so the Mexicans could walk on the inside and not have to be in danger from the car traffic.

Those who do express consternation at the Americans are polite about it at least. There is a restaurant here that refused service in the upstairs dining room to a retired, district attorney friend of mine. The manager told him because he was an American he had to eat downstairs near the kitchen. He informed my friend the upstairs was for Mexican patrons only. And, the manager told him this with the utmost politeness, of course.

When I report these sorts of stories, I usually get many readers' comments that border on the vitriolic. For example, "I've certainly never seen this sort of thing happening anywhere in Mexico and I was once in Puerto Vallarta for two whole weeks." I have even gotten e-mail from Mexicans, not from Central Mexico, who take umbrage at what I write.

The funny thing is the vast majority of Mexicans will never be rude to you in a million years. They will smile and, frankly, patiently endure a lot from Americans (more than they should). But, endure they will.

What gets good in the quest for assimilating to the culture is when you become fluent enough in the language to sit in a home with a local who trusts you enough to tell you things that you will never read in a guidebook or any book about Mexican culture (usually written by an American). He tells you about how he was raised, what he was taught from childhood, and so on.

Nevertheless, when I report what I learned from these encounters, I end up with an inbox full of angry e-mails from those who think they know better — those who live in artificial American-enclave bubbles insulated from Mexican culture. But I keep on, in my not-so-perfect Mexican paradise, learning all I can so I can have more articles to write.

Source: ***www.lasr.net***
Used with permission

United Kingdom

The United Kingdom is a good choice for many who wish to become expatriates because English is the main language. Also, the United States is on good terms with the United Kingdom, so your transition should be much easier than if you wanted to move to somewhere like Russia. A major advantage of becoming a citizen of the United Kingdom is that you are free to work not only in the United Kingdom, but anywhere in the 27 sovereign member states of the European Union. These are Austria, Belgium, Bulgaria, Cyprus, the Czech Republic, Denmark, Estonia, Finland, France, Germany, Greece, Hungary, Ireland, Italy, Latvia, Lithuania, Luxembourg, Malta, the Netherlands, Poland, Portugal, Romania, Slovakia, Slovenia, Spain, Sweden, and of course, the United Kingdom.

If you are not eligible for a European Union passport because you are not a citizen of any of the European Union countries, you still have a good chance of being able to work in the United Kingdom. There is a "Highly Skilled Migrant Program" that grades people based on a point system to ascertain your work value to the United Kingdom. You need 75 total points to be considered eligible, and you can check your eligibility online at the UK Border Agency's Web site **www.ukba.homeoffice.gov.uk/pointscalculator**. This program does not require you to have a specific job lined up, but merely shows that you have skills and are likely to get a job in the United Kingdom. The program is very broad, and awards you points for your age, your ability to speak English, and your experience visiting the United Kingdom. Visit UK Border Agency's Web site **www.workingintheuk.gov.uk** for more information.

The United Kingdom is expensive, but there are jobs for Americans. If nothing else, you could work in a pub. There is no shortage of pub work in England as even the smallest town has at least three pubs, and more often than not pays under the table from £5 to £10 per hour (the equivalent of $8 to $15 USD), depending on where you work. The United Kingdom's climate is one negative to living there. It does not rain as much as many people think, but there are many overcast days. The freedom of movement and lack of government interference with your everyday lives is not the same as it is in the United States. United Kingdom residents do not have our Bill of Rights to protect their privacy. However, it is generally a law-abiding country, and if you stay out of trouble, it is likely that police officials will not take any notice of you.

Gaining citizenship is not too difficult either, and the United Kingdom recognizes dual citizenship. If you live in the United Kingdom for over five years, you may be eligible to be naturalized. If you have British relatives, this may also help your eligibility, especially if they are a parent or grandparent.

The UK Border Agency's Web site provides very clear information about gaining British citizenship at **www.ukba.homeoffice.gov.uk/britishcitizenship/applying**.

Australia and New Zealand

Australia and New Zealand are attractive countries for disappearing individuals, in large part because of their tolerance of others and lack of curiosity about their backgrounds. Many Americans have already moved there, attesting to the popularity of the two countries. Australia's immigration Web site (**www.immi.gov.au**) is comprehensive and easy to navigate and should have the answer to any questions you have, including help with finding the correct the visa or citizenship application. Australia does permit dual citizenship, although it did not before 2002. Australia also has a "Work Holiday" visa specifically for those who are just visiting, but would like to work during that time. However, you need to be between the ages of 18 and 30, show that you have at least $4,700 to support yourself during your stay, and be a high school graduate.

As for New Zealand, its beauty is second to none, and it is often described as a more manageable place to visit in lieu of going to Australia. In other words, it is similar, but it has less people, and it would be harder to get lost in the crowd than in larger Australian cities. It is also not hard to live and work in New Zealand. If you are a skilled worker, you may be able to apply for a job listed on the government "Immediate Skills Shortage List," located at **www.immigration.govt.nz**.

Central America

Many potential expats forget about the other opportunities for relocation on our own continent besides Canada and Mexico. Central America boasts some of the most gorgeous tropical landscapes as well as many opportunities for expatriates. Some think that the quality of life is low in these countries, but many of these assumptions are based on previous decades and are not updated to reflect the improvements many of these countries have made within. The following are some Central American countries to consider when planning your move.

Guatemala

This country has been called the "land of the eternal spring" for its moderate climate. Living is also inexpensive. The country has not only splendid scenery but also a coastline on both the Pacific and the Caribbean. It has tropical forests, mountains, valleys, and mineral springs. Guatemala City is a real urban area, but has a village atmosphere expats enjoy. Plus, North America is close if you decide to return. Fast food chains have long since established a presence, and it generally costs less. Guatemalan food is cheap. There are some crime problems, such as pick-pocketing, in the larger cities. Also, English-language newspapers can be found in most large cities. Domestic help is available at low prices. You can get a live-in house cleaner for $200 a month. Medical and health care is good. If you are willing to work for low pay, there are many jobs. As is true in much of this part of the world, English teaching jobs are generally available.

Nicaragua

Americans do not need a visa to visit Nicaragua, but will have to purchase a $5 tourist card when they arrive. These cards can be valid from 30 to 90 days. Once you are in Nicaragua you may visit its three neighbors, Guatemala, Honduras, and El Salvador, without having to deal with immigration. According to the U.S. Department of State, crime in certain "bad" areas of Nicaragua is common, and police are sparse. You need to have definite street smarts to live in Nicaragua, but the lack of police may be helpful to someone like you who is trying to disappear. There are also many dangers that non-natives may not be aware of, such as stingrays and severe currents in swimming areas, because there are no lifeguards or posted signs. You must research the area you plan to visit thoroughly, and on your own.

The expatriate community in Nicaragua is growing. There are many opportunities for expats to run bed and breakfasts, sailboard charters, adventure tours into the jungle, or any other kind of tourism-related business. Nicaragua is an extremely poor country, possibly the poorest in the Americas along with Haiti, but this means there are many opportunities for growth as well as many government incentives. Amazingly, there are also no foreign restrictions on owning property, so you do not have to become a citizen to live there. There are also special incentives for those who retire to Nicaragua, such as not having to pay any taxes on money made outside the country and the ability to bring up to $20,000 worth of your own stuff duty free into your new home. Even your vehicle is tax exempt up to $25,000, and you can import more vehicles tax-free every five years. You only have to be 45 years old to qualify and provide basic paperwork.

Coldwell Banker® has a division devoted entirely to Nicaragua, and their Web site is **www.cbnicaragua.com**.

Costa Rica

This country has been a hideaway for expats for years. North Americans and Europeans flock to Costa Rica because of its beauty and biodiversity, peaceful life style, stable democratic government, and growing economy. Even with inflation, it is perhaps half as expensive as just about anywhere in North America. If you want some company, it has many expats. You can also choose from among small, medium, and large towns. The country's army was abolished in 1949, and its citizens enjoy such perks as excellent health care and an efficient educational system. Up until 2003, anyone from Canada, the United States, or Panama could enter and exit this country without a passport, though they did need some form of identification, such as a driver's license. In recent years, immigration officials have stepped up efforts, but laws remain lax, and many residents find that if they stay under the radar, they are not likely to be bothered. Anyone who likes the outdoors will almost certainly love this ecologically minded country. With a fast-growing tourist trade, jobs in the tourist business are generally available, often with no questions asked and no visa necessary.

CASE STUDY: JUST BLENDING IN

David Wilkening, author

CLASSIFIED CASE STUDIES™ directly from the experts

In the lobby of a hotel in Costa Rica, I met a very successful photographer in his 30s who left Texas several years ago and headed straight for this country. I asked why here, and he responded, "It's a beautiful place with a laid back lifestyle, and they don't have an army." Costa Rica achieved pacifist heroism when it eliminated its army in the late 1940s.

The photographer's second wife was divorcing him back in the United States. He was losing his only child because his wife was getting custody. He was heavily in debt, and his career was floundering. The photography business was in the doldrums where he lived. "The final straw came when someone stole my credit cards," he said.

This expatriate did not do the intense planning outlined in this book, but he did many of the things mentioned here, such as saving his money before leaving. He also did not tell anyone of his plan. Obviously, he did not have to worry about his stolen credit cards. He sold his old car, which had an auto registration that could trace his whereabouts. He bought a cheap car from a private individual and paid cash to avoid registering the title. When he got to Costa Rica, he formed a plan of escape, but he has never come close to using it. He had money stashed away for emergencies, however.

He has successfully lived in Costa Rica for eight years without being found. Similar to many others, he has found there was no huge effort to find him, though this is not something anyone can count on. He has acquired identification from this country, but he seldom needs it. He wisely also left little trace of his whereabouts when he left. He drove to Costa Rica, so there was no paper trail of airline travel. Costa Rica is about a ten-day drive on the Inter-American Highway from Texas to San Jose, the Costa Rican capitol. Costa Rica is a beautiful country saturated with rainforests and a very diverse flora and flauna. It is also Central

Central America's most advanced nation, socially and economically.

For those reasons, it is not difficult to find Americans who disappeared to start new lives there. Some of them go through the process and become citizens; others simply blend in with the country.

Panama

Panama has a low cost of living and beautiful scenery. Panama is only slightly larger than Florida and is bordered by the Pacific Ocean and the Caribbean Sea. Long stretches of picturesque coastline, lush green valleys, and a mild climate have earned the country the moniker of "the new Florida." English is widely spoken. Panama City is only a little more than a two-hour flight from Miami. Panama has more amenities, lower costs, and less crime than Costa Rica or Mexico. The government's attitude is about as *laissez faire*, a government theory that is opposed to government intervention, as anywhere else on Earth – perfect for anyone who wants to be left alone.

Caribbean

Another area to seriously consider is anywhere in the Caribbean. Keep in mind, however, that each island is different, so you have to factor in your own particular lifestyle considerations. Larger and better-known islands, such as Bermuda and the Caymans, generally have well-organized immigration policies. You might face more risk there upon arrival, but once you have established yourself and your identities, you are probably safer than you would be on smaller islands where everyone knows everyone else. There are many islands to choose from. Some are similar to living in the United States, but others will be a culture shock compared to America.

Although the dream of escaping to a tropical Caribbean island prevails, is it really possible? If you are rich, it is definitely possible, but your dream may not be shattered just because you are not wealthy.

Bermuda & Cayman Islands

The Bermuda and Cayman islands are British territories, which means English is a prominent language. Not only are these islands the very definition of paradise, but they are also favored for their taxing policies. Bermuda is a low-tax country and the Caymans are a tax haven. The Bermuda Islands have payroll taxes and potentially high property taxes but do not tax foreign earnings. In the Cayman Islands, there is no local income or resident taxes, and there is a privacy policy that shields you from having to report any income to the government. You can take your money in or out of the country at will, without penalty.

If you want to gain citizenship, you must keep residency for ten years, which for many is too long to wait. In Bermuda, this makes it nearly impossible for foreigners to own property because there is a 25 percent tax on all foreign-owned homes, which average about $1 million. However, in the Caymans you may purchase real estate without being a citizen. You should not need a visa to visit either Bermuda or the Caymans, as long as you are coming from the United States.

Bermuda's only source of fresh water is rain, which is sometimes too plentiful because it is often in the path of hurricanes. Guns, many types of knives, and ammunition are strictly regulated in Bermuda, and you may not bring any of these with you into the country unless you have special permission from the Bermuda Police Service. The Caymans also have strict rules on weapons, but do not always enforce them like Bermuda does. Both islands enjoy a low to moderate crime rate, so as long as you take standard precautions, such as never leaving luggage unattended and avoiding traveling alone at night, you should be safe.

Cuba

Unless you are one of the very few Americans who fall under the Department of Treasury's Office of Foreign Asset Control's list of exceptions to the U.S. sanctions, you are not going to be able to enter Cuba. A full list of these exceptions is available under Cuba's link in the Country Specific Information page on the U.S. Department of State's Web site (**www.travel.state.gov**), but they mostly cover people who are traveling there because they have close relatives who are citizens of Cuba, or if their profession allows it, such as a photographer or journalist doing some research in Cuba. Even under these circumstances, individuals are not always guaranteed access. However, if you do qualify for access, Cuba should definitely be at the top of your list.

The Cuban government is not going to extradite you if someone comes looking. As long as you obey the rules, and make some effort to learn Spanish, you will probably be left alone. Approximately 5,000 Americans live in Cuba, estimates the U.S. Interests Section, which is the Havana office that acts in place of an embassy. United States and Cuba diplomatic relations ended in 1961. It is a safe country and very private, and Cubans are extremely friendly and helpful.

It would help if you came to Cuba with money because investors are very welcome. The country's 12 million people have a huge, pent-up appetite for goods and services. The country's investment laws encourage foreign businesspeople to own businesses here, as well as homes and offices. You will also have to learn to deal with a socialist economy, but privacy in Cuba allows you to travel worldwide on a Cuban airline with a minimum of information to authorities. This is a country where you can feel safe and secure. You can find out more about Cuba and its government at the U.S. Department of State's Web site at **www.state.gov/r/pa/ei/bgn/2886.htm**.

Cuba does have some disadvantages, though. For one thing, you cannot get there from the United States. You will most likely have to leave via Mexico, Jamaica, the Bahamas, or Canada to avoid travel issues and congestion in Miami. Each year, an estimated 20,000 American tourists do just that, though no one knows how many stay in Cuba. You also cannot use your credit cards there, so you have to bring cash. The biggest problem is finding work. Cuba has many engineers and doctors who work as tour guides because of low pay. If you have money, it is obviously not a problem, but you should not count on being able to support yourself in Cuba.

Dominica

An inexpensive Caribbean island about halfway between Martinique and Guadeloupe, Dominica is a land of waterfalls and rivers (365 of them) and rainforests. It is perhaps the most unspoiled island in the Caribbean without the type of luxury resorts found on more popular islands. There are few direct flights from the United States, so it is somewhat isolated. It is not densely populated, so if you intend to lose yourself in a crowd, you might want to rule it out.

Other Popular Choices Around the Globe

The following are countries that many people have chosen to move to for a variety of reasons.

Ecuador

A little further south into South America is this Nevada-sized country – packed with incredible diversity that includes majestic mountains, lush jungles, mysterious cloud forests, and miles of virtually untouched beaches. Ecuador is packed with small cities undiscovered by tourists. In addition to its natural beauty and low cost, much of the weather in Ecuador is dry with low humidity. This country may cost ⅓ of what it would cost to live in Switzerland or Colorado. Some typical prices include $0.50 for a movie theatre showing films in English, a bus ride for less than $0.10, and a home manicure for less than $1. If you are concerned about language, it is not uncommon for hotels charging less than $250 a week to also offer intense Spanish-language courses.

Increasing numbers of Americans who decide they want to live here can at times find jobs in education. Universities throughout the country are always looking for people with degrees, but a drawback is that outside of teaching, it is not always easy to find anything but menial work.

Portugal

There are hundreds of thousands of expats staying in Spain, but nearby is one of the cheapest countries to live in Europe. An estimated 100,000 expats have found their way here, so there is plenty of company for Americans. The weather is a draw because the further south you head, the hotter the summers with more temperate winters. The beaches are beautiful. In the past, Portugal drew many people because of its low cost of living. It was among the cheapest countries in Europe, but the cost of living has risen in recent years, though it still trails far behind prices found in Great Britain, for example. Business investors from foreign countries are welcome. The country is also known as the easiest Western European country to find work as an English teacher. The pace of life is laid back.

Ireland

This country is popular for many reasons, including its unique combination of storybook scenery coupled with safe streets and a gentle way of life. Much of the country remains pleasantly rural with small farmsteads, quiet lanes, and rolling pasturelands. If you prefer larger cities, Dublin, Ireland's political and financial capital, is a world-class city. It rains often, and even more often, you will find pockets of wind-blown mist. Overall, Ireland is one of the friendliest, safest, and most relaxing countries to live in. It is also a caring society. Hospital treatment is free, and doctors make house calls. This is one of the few countries in the world that can boast a museum for writers. Both writers and artists who can make a living with their work often find this an amiable setting, in part because the country offers various tax breaks to artists of any kind. The high-tech business is also booming, so there are many jobs in that field.

Thailand

The main attraction here has always been the inexpensive cost of living. That is still the case today, but the country itself is also beautiful, with some of the world's best beaches and scenery. Chiang Rai, which is Thailand's northernmost province and its capital, is small but has many of the amenities found in larger cities. It has attracted enough tourists that English-language menus are common. The climate is a major attraction, and Chiang Rai has the country's best climate. The winter months, October through March, are perfect. It rarely rains. Another major advantage is that it is cheap. Some expatriates say they can rent furnished apartments for only $100 a month. Health care is also cheap, as routine doctor visits can cost only $10. There is plenty of recreation as well, with golf courses, government parks, formal gardens, and many hiking trails, although finding an acceptable job is not easy to do in Thailand.

China & Singapore

China is admittedly a big, fast-growing country, but it is highly unlikely you will want to start a new life here. Partly due to a long history of conquest, tourists are all right, but foreigners are not welcome, especially those who want to live there.

However, if you your interest in this country cannot be deterred, you might want to look at Hong Kong and Singapore.

Hong Kong is a booming city with many American companies and jobs represented here. Hong Kong is an excellent place to vanish for many reasons, particularly its large population. Thanks to Great Britain's longtime rule, English is also widely spoken. It has a good strategic geographic location, a well-developed infrastructure, low taxation compared to its competitors, a stable currency, and free-port status. It can be a very good place to live, but the chances are very slim that you will ever find a job here on your own. Most expatriates are here because their home office sent them to Hong Kong. For entrepreneurs who do not have to find a regular job, Hong Kong is a possibility.

Singapore is another city to consider. The city is one of the top when it comes to offshore banking, ranking right up there with Miami, Dubai, and Hong Kong. Recent polls found that while living here is expensive, it is cheaper than Hong Kong.

Singapore has an intriguing blend of Western modernity and Asian culture. It is a safe, modern environment, and unlike much of the rest of Asia, most people here speak English. Singapore is a huge melting pot of international companies and races that create an atmosphere of strong tolerance. The city is safe, clean, and green -- and proud of being one of the original eco-conscious areas of the globe. If you believe in law and order, you will find it in Singapore. Stay away from American bad habits, such as drugs – even chewing some types of gum in public is a crime. In addition to banking, job prospects are possible in importing and exporting. However, establishing residency and other stringent requirements to become a citizen are daunting to many foreigners.

Dubai, United Arab Emirates

Dubai became popular for expats because of tax-free salaries and shopping. The city also is known for having any material item you could possibly want to purchase, allowing for the possibility of a lavish lifestyle. Dubai has established itself as a vital economic force, partly due to its liberal laws, which are a contrast to its more conservative customs. Its major sporting events are drawing ever-larger crowds of tourists, and it has become an extremely international city where only ¼ of the population is native Emiratis.

The major downsides include the high cost of finding a place to live and the culture shock. If you are considering moving to Dubai, learning its laws is paramount. You can be jailed and deported for things like bouncing a check. It is also necessary to respect the Muslim religion, and while you will not be expected to dress like a native, you will have to dress conservatively, especially if you are female. There is also media censorship, so certain Web sites are inaccessible and magazines and television shows are censored.

You can travel to Dubai on a 30-day, non-renewable visa that can be obtained at the airport when you arrive. If you wish to stay longer than 30 days, you should try to find employment before leaving and have your employer take care of the residency and labor visas, which is a common practice. They may also be able to help you get temporary housing. Though you have almost no chance of obtaining citizenship, if you make a good impression with an employer or are recognized as someone who greatly contributes to the society, you may be able to live there on a residency visa for an indefinite amount of time. You can learn more about

Dubai by visiting Dubai's Department of Tourist and Commerce Marketing Web site at **www.dubaitourism.ae**.

Special Considerations When Moving to a New Country

Some people might only chose a new country because it is especially private or has many airports, so getting in and out is a breeze. Here are some special considerations that might influence your decision regarding which country you want to make your new home.

Europe's ocean and seas

If you are worried about exposure, and want to live near water, the Atlantic Ocean borders Spain, Portugal, France, and the United Kingdom, where there are dozens of coastline towns where you can live anonymously, but unless you are looking for a job in the fishing industry, employment is limited. The Mediterranean coast offers much better weather and a growing tourist industry for jobseekers.

Countries with many airports

Some countries are more remote than others, making it difficult to travel back to your home country if necessary. If one of your major concerns is air traffic in and out of a country, Panama should be on your map. It has 100 airports, many of them American built and seldom used, so visitors can fly almost anywhere. Columbia has 504 airports and landing strips, as well as ten international airports. Cuba has 77 airports with paved runaways, and another 94 with dirt roads. Costa Rica has more than 150 airports, Venezuela has more than 250, and Ecuador has 180. In emergencies, you can hire private pilots for only a few hundred dollars to fly you away quickly.

Tax havens

This chapter has mainly been written with an emphasis on people who need to work, but suppose you are among those lucky enough to not need to generate an income. You either have plenty of money or have a regular trust fund or other source of income. If that is your situation, and you want to relocate to another country, you may want to consider moving to a tax haven, a place that enforces little or no taxes.

There are several advantages to relocating to a tax haven. In most countries of the world, residence is the primary basis of taxation. In some places, there are little or no income taxes, but almost all tax havens assess some kind of capital-gains tax or inheritance tax. Some people are unable to return to a country where they used to reside because they are "tax exiles" and are effectively dodging their former country's higher taxes through residency laws of the tax haven. This may only be for a year, or it could be for a certain portion of every year. This is an extremely common thing for rock stars to do in order to avoid being taxed what they feel is an excessive amount. You can guess that many people criticize this move as avoiding taxes that should be paid.

Some individuals hold assets or a trust formed in one tax haven that is usually administered in another country. The idea is to hold assets, such as real estate, and change the ownership in a lower tax jurisdiction. This method is often employed to avoid a specific tax. A well-off owner might transfer his or her house to an offshore company so he or she can file a trust fund. On the death of the holder, the shares go to a relative who receives the house without having to pay an inheritance tax.

Various businesses prefer to set up in tax havens because they do not require specific locations. Many reinsurance companies, for example, have migrated to Bermuda in recent years. Internet-based companies and group finance businesses have also used this option. This is sometimes known as "re-invoicing," which means companies make a profit margin without performing any economic function, but because the "margin" came in a tax-free country, it allowed the owner to take profits from the high-end jurisdiction.

One example, as mentioned earlier in this chapter, is the Cayman Islands, which have highly favorable tax and bankruptcy laws and easy access to U.S. financial markets. The small islands have long been a hot bed for alternative investments.

You can find additional resources relating to tax havens in the Appendix of this book.

Housing in foreign countries

Foreign countries usually have different rules, and housing often involves apartments. Buying an apartment in any foreign country can be a complicated process. There are many potential obstacles and traps for anyone without knowledge of local customs and practices. The likelihood of making a serious mistake will decrease if you have sufficient information about the market and local customs.

The relative instability of some countries compared to the United States is also a cause for concern when looking at living arrangements. In Thailand, the entire law related to foreigners buying homes and other property was changed after a public uproar over the prime minister using a loophole to avoid paying his taxes. The changing of the law forced out many foreigners, including Americans, who were otherwise going to buy homes. The new law effectively prohibits foreigners from full ownership.

Using Professional Help to Relocate

Due to these various complications, it is highly recommended that if you decide to move there, you should hire an attorney or firm that specializes in helping expats relocate. These experts can assist you with documentation and possibly finding work or housing depending on the type of professional you hire. You should be able to find a firm that is sensitive to your desire for privacy.

Here are some tips on evaluating potential expatriate consultants:

- Determine whether a consultant is discreet and can be counted on to do as much for you as possible without using your identity.
- Find someone focused on your needs, not theirs. They should be asking questions about you, though you will

have to be selective in how much you want to reveal to them.

- Check references, of course, and see how many Americans the firm has counseled.
- Make sure they are truly independent. Some of these firms are beholden to local vendors and cannot give you truly independent opinions.
- Part-time consultants will perhaps charge less, but this is too important a matter for anything other than an established firm.

Here are some of the most useful Web sites for expatriates looking for places to live and other information:

- AsiaXPAT (**www.asiaxpat.com**): Provides information for expats and professionals living and working in Asia.
- Clickflatshare.com (**www.clickflatshare.com**): A free resource for finding and posting ads for housing in Europe, Australia, New Zealand, and Asia.
- EscapeArtist.com (**www.escapeartist.com**): A complete resource for starting a new life abroad, with information on finding overseas real estate, jobs, and more.
- ExpatExchange (**www.expatexchange.com**): Helps expats navigate relocation and the phases of culture shock.
- Expat World (**www.expatworld.net**): An electronic version of the Expat World Newsletter, providing dozens of articles and information on products to aid in relocating.

- Expatica (**www.expatica.com**): Provides daily news, features, and practical information on living abroad in Europe.
- The Expatriate Café (**www.expatriatecafe.com**): A site for expatriates living and teaching English in Spain.
- Expatriates.com (**www.expatriates.com**): A community Web site created for and by expatriates and internationally minded people everywhere.

chapter 5

Moving to Your New Life

You can leave town however you wish, but a taxi service is not recommended. Drivers and their dispatchers take records of everyone picked up and dropped off. Taxi drivers may also recognize you if questioned. Even if it is unlikely anyone is going to seriously pursue you, it is best not to take any chances.

Leaving town by automobile does not involve buying a ticket or using additional documentation of your identity, but it can provide investigators with a trace to you through licensing records. If possible, it is a good idea to leave the car behind. Sell it long before you leave, or abandon it.

If you are leaving town by car, it is not a good idea to have all your belongings in the back seat. If a police officer stops you for a routine traffic check, he or she might conclude the obvious — you are moving. He or she may not know the circumstances involved, but you do not want to raise any suspicions.

If you stay in a hotel, be sure to scrub every surface with soap and water so as not to leave fingerprints or skin cells. Police technicians will probably not be checking for this type of evidence because you are likely not a criminal, but if a trained, well-financed investigator is on your trail, he or she might find clues. Do not leave any.

Moving Concerns

Here are six tips for maintaining your new identity while moving:

1. When you are changing houses or apartments, do not leave behind items that might be traceable to you. These include items that indicate your interests, hobbies, and lifestyle. Consider your books, for example.

2. Just as you never want to send change-of-address forms to magazines or other periodicals, you do not want to leave a similar document at the local post office. Your mail will be returned to senders, stamped with something like this: "Moved; left no forwarding address." This may not discourage determined sleuths who want to find you, but it will put off casual lookers.

3. If you need help moving, hire some "no name" company from another city or hire locals who are not part of a moving company that could furnish investigators a lead to your next whereabouts. If you want to be safe, put your things in public storage and then move again later to wherever you are living. Also, give fictitious information to agents renting the space.

4. Avoid getting friendly with your new landlord. Hold up your end of the rental agreement, and he or she will be happy to leave you alone. Remember landlords are good sources of information for snoopy people. Watch carefully what you say to them, and do not leave personal tips that can lead to your discovery.

5. Keep in mind also that if you do not pay your rent and skip out the landlord will be motivated to help find your new address.

6. Before you move, cancel or let lapse any life insurance you have. If there is any cash value, take the money before you leave. Insurance companies are good gatherers of personal information; be sure not to leave tips with your current agent on any of your plans. Give them believable excuses.

It takes an enormous amount of time and effort to disappear, and if you make that decision, there is a long list of things not to do in your new life. Many of these are simple, everyday matters that are part of a life's routine and are barely given a second thought.

If you are leaving, here are just a few of the things you should not do in your new life:

- Attend your place of worship. Members may delve into your background, and the less people know, the better.
- Stay in touch with old neighbors. Isolate yourself from them. You cannot afford friendship.
- Drive recklessly or bother new neighbors. You want to avoid the authorities at all costs.

- Maintain your life insurance policies. They leave a paper trail for others to find you. Let them lapse.
- Have products delivered to your doorstep. This might give your address away in the future.

It is getting more difficult all the time to live and travel anonymously without leaving some kind of trail. Furthermore, in large part because air travel is the fastest way to get between countries, it is even more difficult to travel the world than it is to move within North American confines.

The first rule when considering travel is that you do not want to leave a credit card or check trail behind you.

Travel by Plane

If you know that the police will look for you, taking a plane is the least secretive means of travel because each flight has a passenger roster. Airport security has heightened since Sept. 11. Though you are obviously not a terrorist, you still should be cautious if you choose to fly to your new home. Airports are crammed with security cameras, and you will end up on film. If the police search for you, they will be allowed access to that footage. Also, if you are pulled aside for a more thorough bag or body inspection, more people will notice you. Check the Transportation Security Administration's (TSA) Web site (**www.tsa.gov**) and be sure you are not traveling with anything that is prohibited. The TSA is responsible for the security of all modes of transportation, including screening passengers and their baggage while traveling into and out of U.S. airports. Although many weapons are permitted in checked baggage, anything that has the potential to be explosive is not allowed in checked bags. This includes simple items, such as matches and bleach.

You also need to prove your identity. Accepted forms of ID according to the TSA are:

- U.S. passport
- U.S. passport card
- DHS "Trusted Traveler" cards (NEXUS, SENTRI, FAST)
- U.S. Military ID (active duty or retired military and their dependents)
- Permanent Resident Card
- Border Crossing Card
- DHS-designated enhanced driver's license
- Drivers Licenses or other state photo identity cards issued by Department of Motor Vehicles (or equivalent) that meets REAL ID benchmarks (All states are currently in compliance)
- A Native American Tribal Photo ID
- An airline or airport-issued ID (if issued under a TSA-approved security plan)
- A foreign government-issued passport
- Canadian provincial driver's license or Indian and Northern Affairs Canada (INAC) card
- Transportation Worker Identification Credential (TWIC)

The TSA Web site states: "Passengers who do not or cannot present an acceptable ID will have to provide information to the Transportation Security Officer performing Travel Document Checking duties in order to verify their identity. Passengers who are cleared through this process may be subject to additional screening."

Many people on various travel blogs have noticed their boarding passes are tagged with the code "SSSS," and they are pulled aside for additional screening. Some say this is completely random, while others insist there are "markers" that will get you labeled with this "Secondary Security Screening Selection" code. TSA has not made any official statements about this, but just in case, it cannot hurt to avoid some of the supposed markers for being selected for extra screening. These include:

- Paying for you ticket in cash
- Purchasing a one way ticket
- Purchasing your ticket the same day as your flight
- Skipping a leg of your flight if it has stopovers
- Not having your ID

Never try to fool airport security. You will be arrested and likely face extremely hefty fines. TSA has a blog on their Web site where they discuss some of the ways people attempt to manipulate the system, how they fail, and what happened to them.

Travel by Bus

Although taking a bus will take longer than a more direct method, such as a plane or driving yourself, the bus is a great option if you are traveling light and want to save some money. Bus tickets are far cheaper than any other form of travel. Greyhound is the only bus company that has routes throughout the United States, as well as Mexico and Canada. There are many smaller companies that work with Greyhound to expand their service area. You can visit Greyhound's Web site (**www.greyhound.com**) or call 1-800-231-2222 for more information. You can book tickets online, but this will create a record in its system that may be searched if officials are looking for you. Instead, purchase your ticket at the station in cash. You will still need your ID, but there is no official passenger roster like airlines have.

While bus travel is not known to be the safest, is has greatly improved over the years. As long as you are a smart traveler and do not wear expensive clothing or jewelry, or leave your luggage unattended, you should be fine.

Travel by Train

While Amtrak (**www.amtrak.com**) is the most common and well-known train company in the United States, there are other trains, many of which run on daily basis. Trains offer some wonderful benefits for travelers that most disregard in favor of speed. Yes, you may be traveling overnight to your destination, but you are free to get up and walk around, you can request a sleeping car and actually get some rest, and many of the train routes in the United States are scenic. You can also bring up to 250 pounds of baggage onto the train — two carry-on bags and three checked bags all at 50 pounds. There is no way to get that much onto a bus or airplane as a lone traveler.

Trains also have fairly fixed rates regardless of what day of the week it is, and there are only some changes for the busier holiday times. Last-minute purchases are common, so they will not appear strange. At IndependentTraveler.com, there is a listing of the major train routes besides Amtrak's, which include the Ethan Allen Express from New York to Vermont, the Crescent from New York to New Orleans, and the Coast Starlight, which travels from Los Angeles to Seattle.

Travel by Houseboat or RV

Traveling by water is not an immediately obvious means of transportation; therefore, it is one of the best ways to stay hidden while traveling in North America. Part of the reason North America is perfect for this type of travel is the many waterways available. There are the Great Lakes and many other bodies of water on the Mississippi or the Atlantic Intracoastal Waterways. Depending on your method of disappearing, you can rent a houseboat or other type of boat. Of course, hiring someone to drive your boat leaves a trail. You can learn to operate the boat by yourself, but you will need certain skills, including:

- The ability to read nautical charts
- An understanding of buoys and other water markers
- Knowledge about what to do in adverse weather
- The ability to fix your boat if something breaks down, which includes mechanical and electrical skills
- The ability to recognize and avoid various natural hazards, such as sand bars or waterfalls

- An understanding of what signs might lead to an adverse change in weather, such as a drop in temperature

For those who do not want a permanent address, houseboats are good investments. They have all the living amenities you might want. You do not normally need any kind of boating license to operate a houseboat. They are also ideal for rigging for a quick escape. Medium-sized houseboats are also inconspicuous and not easily identified.

If you prefer land, a small, ordinary recreational vehicle or RV is another practical way to get around discreetly. If you go this route, buy from a private owner, not a dealer, so you can avoid filling out paperwork that might leave a trace. You will also want to pay cash, which arouses far less suspicion when dealing with an individual than with a large company.

One advantage of RVs is the freedom to stay off major highways and take side roads. The best method is to stick to secondary roads instead of interstates and other main highways, as RVs can be easily broken into, so you should also buy some reinforced locks.

Camping

Depending on your time constraints, the best way to get from point A to point B might be to travel outdoors by foot. Depending on the route you choose for your escape, it might take a while, and you have to be in reasonably good shape. One route might be the Appalachian Trail in the east because it stretches over 2,000 miles from Georgia to Maine.

This might not be the most appropriate way of getting around for most North American trips, but you might consider it under special circumstances. If this is the method that best suits you, you should probably buy the necessary hiking and camping equipment and do part of your trip in the woods. Even if someone knows you are hiking, it is almost impossible to determine where you got off the trail and switched to another form of transportation.

Hitchhiking is also an option, but few motorists these days pick up people with their thumbs in the air. It is potentially dangerous, not only for the motorist, but also for the hitchhiker. You never know who is going to pick you up or what kind of driver he or she may turn out to be. If you are considering traveling this way, you might want to keep hitchhiking in mind, though.

Moving Your Money to Your New Home

Now you should know how to get yourself to your new home, but what about your money? You may encounter some issues you did not anticipate. Your money and your identity are inextricably linked, so you need to be careful where you put it and who knows it belongs to you. You should also be aware that transactions in the amount of $10,000 or more are reported to the IRS via Form 8300. The IRS defines these transactions as:

- Sale of goods, services, or real or tangible property
- Rental of goods or real or personal property
- Cash exchanged for other cash

- Establishment, maintenance of, or contribution to a trust or escrow account
- A loan repayment
- Conversion of cash to a negotiable instrument, such as a check or a bond

If you are trying to get your money out of this country and into your new home somewhere else in the world, there are many alternatives to get your assets out of the United States. One of your first acts should be to find a friendly banker or lawyer. This depends, though, on where you are headed. Almost all the Caribbean Islands, and most of the Central American communities, have a strong, long-established banking structure. In Belize, there are familiar names, such as Barclay's Bank and the Bank of Nova Scotia.

Many countries, including the United States, discourage such asset movement. The simplest way to get your money out is to carry it yourself. You can only take $10,000 per person when you leave the United States. You might get friends to help, but you do not want to violate the law, so you must stick to $10,000 a trip. This could require a few trips, but cash leaves few trails.

Driving your money to your new home

If your new destination is Mexico or anywhere south of the United States, you might consider putting your money in your car and driving there. Do not take a substantial amount of money all in one trip. Some people have been known to hire professionals who make a living running caravans to countries such as Mexico and Costa Rica. These entrepreneurs carry groups of people for a fee. They do not advertise, so you have to find them by word of mouth, but there is nothing illegal in your hiring personal "body-guards" to help you move your money.

Another possibility for moving money is to wire it to a foreign account or corporation you have set up. This is a somewhat complicated process, and you would be wise to find an expert on the subject.

The U.S. government severely restricts your movement of money. Officially, it is done to fight money laundering, or even terrorism. In this area, you might want to get some expert advice, but there are some broad suggestions.

Opening a new bank account

It is difficult to open a bank account without a social security number, but because there are no such federal requirements, you can argue with a banker. You can remind them there are no federal statutes requiring banks to get social security numbers. The government does require banks to make an effort to secure customer numbers for certain interest-bearing accounts. Parts of the federal law specifically exclude a bank's necessity to even make the effort to report social security numbers for certain accounts.

You would be legally on the right side of this issue, and you might win a short argument with banking officials. If you are trying to keep a low profile and live entirely on your new IDs, though, it is not a good idea to fight bank bureaucrats who might want a social security number. They might think of you later in case anyone ever comes checking. Find another bank if you have trouble. Remember that even though banks are not required by the government to get a social security number, the bank might have an internal policy about obtaining social security numbers.

If you have trouble opening a bank account in your new name with the identification you have, there are alternatives. One is online banking, but for someone worried about identity, think of the implications — no face-to-face involvement with tellers or anyone else. Some banks will allow you to apply for an account by telephone. Many of these banks offer free checking with no monthly maintenance fees. Some of these offers involve free credit cards and even discounts on eyewear.

Another alternative to exposing yourself by banking in person is opening an account through the mail. Simply send a letter to a bank saying you are moving to the area and want to open an account. You use your mail drop as a return address. Getting a banker to be more relaxed and perhaps forget the requirement of a social security number may be easier if you can establish a relationship with someone. It doesn't hurt to hint that you will be depositing large sums of money with their institution, either.

How to find bank procedures

A simple way to find out the different procedures at various banks is to open an account in your real name with your previous identification. You might also consider going with a friend and seeing the procedures when he or she opens an account.

Just how much and what type of information you will need to open a bank account in the United States varies according to each bank. Small banks in rural areas usually have lower threshold requirements than larger banks in urban areas. Bankers are not supposed to be influenced by the amount of your deposit, but they are. If you are investing a large amount, it is possible a banking representative might be inclined to let some required paperwork be uncompleted or even left out entirely. You cannot count on this, of course, but it is possible.

Almost all banks follow a specific formula for opening new accounts. When opening an account, you should be prepared to provide basic information such as your name, birthday, and driver's license. There is always the chance the bank will ask for a copy of your social security card as well. If you do not want to provide it, you might be able to "fudge" on this by saying you have just ordered a new card and you have yet to receive it by mail, but that you will provide it later. The bank official may not remember this detail, and you may get away with the omission. If the banker is insistent, the best course of action is to try another institution. You might also consider looking at the institution's Web site before going in person to open an account to see what type of information is required.

You should be aware of the Bank Secrecy Act, which has been around since the 1930s, with many modifications. Under recent revisions, it authorizes the Treasury Department to require any financial institution to report any "suspicious transaction relevant to a possible violation of law or regulations." That means that each deposit, withdrawal, currency exchange, or other payment transfer of more than $10,000 will be reported to the U.S. Treasury Department, and you will be required to fill out information regarding your identity, the reasons for the currency exchange, and the source of the money.

Problems with your bank account

A frozen bank account is an account that you cannot access because someone – usually a creditor – has placed a hold on it. When your bank account is frozen, you can put money into it, but you cannot withdraw it. A creditor or debt collector cannot freeze your account unless it has a judgment from a court. If they win, they will be awarded a writ of judgment, which in most states can be used to garnish the debtor/defendant's bank account.

The simple way to avoid this is to diversify. Do not put all your money in one account. This may be tempting to some because the more money you have in one savings account, the more interest you will earn. This is a major advantage an average person may seen in holding only one account, but you are not the average person. Be sure some of your money is in another place. Also, never have a safety deposit box in the same bank you use for checking.

Living sans-checking account

With some creative thinking, you might get along fine without a bank or checking account. For example, you could pay your bills by money order. However, it can be difficult in today's world where most things, even in many foreign countries, are paid for using credit cards.

Cash, unlike credit cards or checking accounts, is untraceable. Personal checks leave a paper trail and are increasingly viewed with distrust; credit cards also leave a paper trail. If you happen to be fleeing an abusive spouse whose name is on the account, he or she can simply cancel the cards.

There are many benefits to using cash, but common sense comes into play here as well. If you purchase a new $40,000 car and pay cash, a car dealer will most likely assume you are linked to criminal activity. However, when dispensed in small amounts, cash is the best way to continue your anonymity.

Perth Mint

The Perth Mint (**www.perthmint.com.au**) sells coins and precious metals for investment purposes. The actual Perth Mint is in Australia, but there are authorized dealers throughout the world that deal with Perth Mint. Dealers located in the United States are:

- Asset Strategies International, Inc: Based in Maryland. **www.assetstrategies.com**

- Euro Pacific Capital, Inc: Main office is in Connecticut, but they have branch offices in New York, Florida, Arizona, and California. **www.europac.net**

Perth Mint holds your coins or metals and issues you a certificate that states you are rightful owner. Perth Mint certificates are easy to liquidate, and precious metal values tend to be more stable than the dollar. If you are leaving the country, you may feel much more secure traveling with the certificate rather than a large amount of cash. However, you are required to make an initial purchase of $10,000 to be involved in the Perth Mint Certificate Program (PMCP), so the 8300 form would be filed with the IRS.

Swiss annuities

You may also take advantage of investing money in Switzerland, but you will need at least $25,000 to start investing. There are many benefits to Swiss annuities, including the fact that you do not have to report them to the IRS because it is not considered a bank account, but an insurance contract. You must speak with a professional financial advisor who has experience with Swiss annuities to ensure you understand all the implications of your investment. Be selective when it comes to finding an advisor. Volcon (**www.volcon.ch**) is a reputable company based in Switzerland that can help set up Swiss annuities. The International Financial and Legal Network (**www.ifln.com**) can also help you understand the laws between countries and how to invest abroad.

Banking in Switzerland

Banking in Switzerland is characterized by stability, privacy, and protection of clients' assets and information. The country's tradition of bank secrecy, which dates to the Middle Ages, was first codified in a 1934 law. All banks in Switzerland are regulated by Swiss Financial Market Supervisory Authority (FINMA), which derives its authority from a series of federal statutes. It is estimated that ⅓ of all funds held outside the country of origin (sometimes called "offshore" funds) are kept in Switzerland.

Swiss bank secrecy does not protect private banking information; the protections afforded under Swiss law are similar to confidentiality protections between doctors and patients or lawyers and their clients. The Swiss government views the right to privacy as a fundamental principle that should be protected by all democratic countries. Although secrecy is protected, in practice, all bank accounts are linked to an identified individual, and a prosecutor or judge may issue a "lifting order" to grant law enforcement access to information relevant to a criminal investigation.

Swiss bank accounts cannot be opened without the holder signing a legal document asserting that they have no outstanding financial obligations to the IRS. Despite this, Swiss banks have been criticized for improperly shielding individuals practicing tax evasion. Because only tax fraud — actively lying to authorities — is a crime in Switzerland, while tax evasion — passively neglecting to report income — is not, it is believed that many tax evaders have been able to take advantage of the Swiss privacy provisions.

In January 2003, the United States Department of Treasury announced a new information-sharing agreement under the already existing U.S.-Swiss Income Tax Convention; the agreement was intended to facilitate more effective tax information exchanges between the two countries. However, Swiss policy has continued to come under international criticism. In March 2009, Switzerland agreed to renegotiate more effective tax cooperation with the United States and other countries.

Some bank accounts are afforded an extra degree of privacy. Information concerning such accounts, known as numbered accounts, is restricted to senior bank officers, rather than being accessible by all employees of a bank. However, the information required to open such an account is no different from that of an ordinary account; completely anonymous accounts are not allowed by law. Should a criminal investigation take place, law enforcement has access to information related to a numbered account in the same way it has access to information about any other account.

According to Swiss law, nonresidents who would like to open a bank account must be at least 18 years old. This is one of the only restrictions. Your account can be in almost any currency, including the U.S. dollar, and there is usually no minimum balance required to open an account. Find out more about opening a Swiss account by visiting the HowStuffWorks Web site at **http://money.howstuffworks.com/personal-finance/banking/swiss-bank-account.htm.**

Hawala banking

Although Swiss banking is the most well-known, Hawala banking is another ancient banking system you might consider using. Hawala banking is one of the oldest systems in existence, and because there is no actual money movement, it cannot be traced. Unfortunately, it has been linked to the world of terrorism, but that was never its original purpose and many people who have no ill or illegal intentions still use it today. Despite its dubious reputation, and its role in money laundering, it has another side. "It's used around the world to conduct legitimate remittances," says Interpol. Any attempts by the United States and other governments to curb it are doomed to fail, according to an analysis by the International Monetary Fund.

Hawala banking developed in India before the introduction of Western business practices. It is attractive to vanishers because there are no written documents, and exchanges are based on mutual trust. No real money crosses the border.

This hypothetical situation is one example of a transfer: A New York cab driver has saved $1,000 that he wants to send to relatives in Spain. He tries to do it through a bank, which would prefer he open an account before doing business with them. Even if he does that, though, he will be charged a high fee. Mail there is not dependable and can take weeks to arrive, so the cab driver talks to a bartender he knows, who is an unofficial member of Hawala. This man will arrange delivery through a third party, charging our cab driver a delivery charge and a commission fee. He finds a mutual acquaintance who will hand over the money to the cab driver's relatives. Because the Hawala members deal with each other on a regular basis they just keep a ledger of their transactions so they know how much money they are owed or owe at all times. Even the most casual observer of this system can see immediately that trust plays a heavy role in its success, and that it is inherently risky.

chapter 6

Changing Your Body and Mind

By disappearing, you are abandoning your old life – and the old you as well. You need to re-create your appearance and the way you present yourself to people. This has a two-fold purpose, one being the obvious need to disguise yourself, and the other perhaps less considered is your mental health. No matter how horrible your old life may have been, it will be hard to let go of everything you knew and loved. You can use this transitionary period to your advantage and try things you always wanted to do before, but could not due to expectations forced upon you in your old life. This can help you remain positive and feel comfortable in your new life. It will also give you some closure in moving on from your past.

Altering Your Appearance

Changing how you look is an important way to keep anyone from identifying you. People who knew you before you disappeared will recognize you, and those looking for you will inquire, with a picture of the old you, "Have you seen this person?" Your main goal when it comes to changing your appearance is to look natural. If you look like you are hiding something, such as a person wearing an obvious wig and dark sunglasses, you will stick out. Just like the story of your new life, you appearance and attitude should be bland. Once your new identity is well established, you can expand your look and your social circle, but initially you will want to lay low. The following sections offer suggestions for changing your appearance.

Hair

You can cut, dye, or cover your hair. If you have long hair, cut it shorter. Women who have always had plain hairstyles can get a cut that requires more maintenance, such as layers. Men can give themselves the appearance of a receding hairline, which may not be the most appealing, but will definitely help alter their appearance. If cost is an issue, many training salons offer services for extremely low prices, possibly even for free. You can also cover your hair with a wig or toupee, but good ones are often hundreds of dollars. Do not bother with any hairpiece that is not convincing. They can be distracting and usually look silly, meaning these looks will be memorable.

Eyes

Colored contacts are hit or miss when it comes to believability. On some people, they look very natural, but on others it is obvious they are fake. The best way to tell is to make an appointment with an optometrist to try them on. You can also purchase them from a Web site, such as CoastalContacts.com. However, if you have never been fitted for contacts you can damage your eyes by wearing a pair that is ill-suited for your eyes. You can purchase colored contacts whether or not you need vision correction. A better option may be purchasing glasses. Glasses will change your look much more than contacts and are far cheaper and easier to maintain. If you normally wear contacts, switch to glasses, and vice versa.

Changing your eyebrow shape will also help change your face. Yes, men can pluck their eyebrows too. You can do this yourself or go to a salon, where it usually costs about $10. However, do not become a regular at any salon and rotate the establishments you visit as much as possible.

Teeth

Teeth whitening is very popular today, and strips bought at any drugstore are surprisingly effective and not too expensive. They range from $15 to $40 a box and the process takes one to two weeks to complete. If you normally smile often and show your teeth, try to do so less often, or smile more if you normally do not. Practice making facial expressions in a mirror to be sure you are not making strange faces until you are comfortable with your new expressions.

There are other options, such as professional teeth whitening, veneers, and braces, but the cost of these options is not likely worth the change to your appearance unless you have the money and truly want to go through the procedure. If you do wish to undergo these procedures, you will need to visit a dentist. Also, do not cease to take care of your teeth in order to change your appearance. Hopefully no one would consider this, but it should be mentioned that health should come before you looks.

Skin

You might decide to get some more sun for a darker complexion or stay indoors more to lighten your skin tone. But stay away from spray tans or makeup to change your skin tone. Focus more on changing marks on your skin such as freckles, moles, scars, and tattoos. If the mark is particularly unique, you can pay to have it removed. Tattoos are the most obvious, especially if they are visible while wearing clothing. People do not forget elaborate tattoos, and this could be an easy way of recognizing you.

Tattoos are most commonly removed with lasers. Unfortunately, tattoo removal is impossible to guarantee and can be very expensive and painful. If the ink is fairly new, was injected unevenly into your skin, or is a brand that is harder to remove, you will be stuck with a faded tattoo. This could be even more memorable, so use discretion in this matter. Scar removal is also done with a laser, and can also cost hundreds of dollars an hour. Prices for all of these procedures vary very much on a case-by-case basis. A larger scar or tattoo will obviously cost more to remove than a smaller one, and certain people may have sensitive skin that will require special considerations, such as more treatments that are shorter in length rather than a couple longer sessions.

Getting moles removed is quick, virtually painless, and not that expensive. Emphasize to your dermatologist that you really want there to be as little evidence of the mole left as possible so he or she takes the time to get as much as possible to avoid scarring.

There are many home remedies for lightening freckles; however, results will vary. The best thing you can do for freckles is limit sun exposure.

Makeup

Women who want a new look can visit most makeup counters and ask for suggestions on a new look and receive a free makeover. This is a great way to get an idea of how to change your look and get someone else's opinion at the same time. Remember to aim for a natural and believable look, so vibrant colors should generally be avoided. Men can also use small amounts of makeup to hide distinguishing marks.

Clothing and accessories

Also change your personal hygiene products, including shampoo, conditioner, deodorant, and perfume or cologne so your smell is different. This may seem overly cautious, but if the police suspect you were kidnapped, they might send scent dogs on your trail. Also, you just never know when you could bump into an old acquaintance that may recognize your smell. Someone who may have otherwise walked right past you could stop in their tracks when they smell your signature perfume or cologne.

Throw out your old wardrobe. Go native and dress as the locals do. In tropical climates, that means casual and simple. Buy your new clothes locally to help make yourself feel a part of the community and to blend in with everybody else living there.

Surgery

If you truly want to alter your appearance, consider getting plastic surgery just before embarking on your new life. It used to be costly, but with new advances in medicine and new techniques, the price can be affordable. Dozens of clinics in recent years have opened in countries such as Mexico, Honduras, and Costa Rica for people wanting more affordable face lifts, tucks, and body sculpting. You may be wary of trusting a surgeon across the border, but an investigation of the doctor should reveal where you can get competent care. U.S. doctors might be of help in recommending someone.

What if You are Recognized?

What do you do if a childhood friend recognizes you in the street or if someone recognizes you from a "have you seen this person" flyer? The odds are certainly against this happening, but you should be prepared for it. If you encounter someone who did not know you well, you can often bluff your way through a conversation, saying that you are someone else and are not familiar with the person. If you have another identification card, you might even consider showing the person proof of your other identity. It is likely you can persuade casual friends that you are not who they think you are, particularly if you put on a convincing act.

The situation here also depends on how much time has passed. If someone last saw you two years ago, for example, that is a very different situation than if you were not in contact for 25 years. If you encounter someone who knew you well and perhaps has not seen you for only a few years, in all likelihood, the denial will probably not work.

If you are living in a large city, however, you might acknowledge that it is indeed you and then ask for your friend's telephone number and address to avoid giving out your own or give the person a fake number. You can say you will call to "catch up on old times," but do not actually follow through. Because you are living in a big city, it is unlikely you will run into another chance encounter with an old acquaintance.

If you live in a small city, of course, the situation is different because you are likely to come in contact with the person again in the future. However, at this point, you still have options. You can tell the friend the truth about why and how you ran away. Doing so involves trust, of course, but it is one of your options. Even if you divulge the truth of your situation, keep in mind that there is probably no reason your friend will want to expose your whereabouts. However, a friend might tell another friend. Soon, your whereabouts are common knowledge to those you left behind. Perhaps you do not want to take that risk, in which case, another option is to relocate again.

chapter 7

Finding a New Job

There are essentially two options for employment in your new life. You can find a job in some field where you have expertise, such as engineering, or, if you are entrepreneurial-minded, you can start your own business. It is far easier to remain anonymous as a salaried employee, but there are ways to secretly run a home-based business as well. Something to consider, whatever your choice, is that the best form of employment for your case is often not the highest paid, but something that allows you to remain anonymous.

Go Back to School

If you have limited work experience and independent wealth, you might be in a position to go back to college or to a technical school to learn a new profession or trade. Because financial assistance through the government is not a good option if you are trying to remain anonymous, you must have a source of cash to pay for classes or certifications.

Some colleges offer tests to receive credit for knowledge you already have, regardless of where you obtained it, called the College-Level Examination Program® (CLEP) tests in the United States. This can help you avoid taking unnecessary classes, but these tests cost money — $77 through the College Board. In addition, after you register with a college, you may be given a variety of placement tests. This is particularly true in colleges that specialize in music, the arts, or engineering. Some off-campus colleges also grant credit based on your presentation of a portfolio. To earn a humanities credit for an off-campus class in art, for example, you might have to bring in a portfolio of your oil paintings to a professor and explain the work.

Another option available at some colleges — particularly community colleges — is to earn credit by watching selected public broadcasting television programs. You will most likely have to take a test, but you can do this at home. There are also college correspondence courses. This is another distant-learning option where you study materials via e-mail and send back your answers to the school. An increasing number of colleges are also offering online courses. With a computer, a phone connection, and Internet service, you can work at anywhere and anytime.

Anonymous Occupations

Your first job as a "vanisher" may have to be something basic and mundane. It may take a while to establish your new identity, and you might not have many choices when it comes to work. A good choice if you can do it, however, is day labor. The work can be labor intensive and is restricted to men to some extent, but many places pay cash, and most people do not care about your background. You should be able to raise enough money as a day laborer to keep yourself fed and housed.

If you have previous experience using cameras or have worked with a photographer in the past, consider starting your own photography business. Photography, like any skill, is in high demand. Being self-employed and able to use a camera can provide a steady source of income and only a relatively small initial investment is needed to get started. All your gear, for example, can be purchased used in a pawnshop. In addition to shooting pictures for magazines as a freelance photographer or the booming wedding business, many photographers find that selling stock photos to companies who use generic photos for a variety of uses is a good side business. If you sell your photos directly, you have no middleman and can count on being anonymous because few companies care who shot the pictures.

If you happen to live near the ocean, consider taking up an occupation that is sea-related. There are people who make a decent living by digging clams, harvesting sea urchins, and gathering worms for fishermen — occupations many do not think about. Another related field is to become a commercial angler. If you happen to live near a yacht club with fancy boats, still another area of gainful employment is to start a boat cleaning business. These fields often involve cash payments, so you avoid checks and other methods of payment that might involve identification. You are also your own boss in these occupations, so you can come and go as quietly as you please.

If you are artistically inclined, consider becoming an artist and selling your work at art festivals, tourist strips, vacation spots, and county fairs. People come and go without attracting much notice in areas of heavy tourism, which will help maintain anonymity. To preserve their identity, some artists represent themselves as agents rather than artists. They show their own work, but often under a different name.

Becoming a musician is another occupation that allows for anonymity. Local music industries are largely unregulated and too small to attract the attention of government officials. Nobody cares who you are, and there are seldom any questions about your background. Most musicians also are part of a cash market, so this is often a way to stay away from the IRS. Please note, however, that it is illegal to make money over a certain amount in the United States and not report it to the IRS to pay taxes on that money.

You might also want to consider getting into the apartment locating business. There is demand everywhere for people who can help potential tenants find housing. If you want to do this on your own rather than working for someone else, you can run an ad and accumulate a file on prospective tenants and what they are looking for. You can then help potential renters find housing that matches their needs and charge a per hour or per person fee for your service.

If you have prior mechanical abilities, another attractive business is auto repair. Mechanics earn a good living, and because they are in demand, potential employers may not look at their background. Some employers simply want mechanics to prove their skills to get the job. You can also consider starting your own repair business. You will need access to tools and equipment, but through word-of-mouth marketing, you may be able to run a profitable business if you can prove your skill.

The need of identification and references in any particular job highly depends on the company you are trying to gain employment with. In informal situations, you may be able to get away with not having these documents. The following are other occupations that are desirable, in part because of convenient anonymity:

- Become a skilled carpenter — particularly if you are in an area that has an increasing population and, thus, homes, apartments, and condominiums. Carpenters are in demand virtually everywhere, and again, ID or references are not usually required once you show you can do the work in informal situations.

- Become a gardener or work for a lawn service. You can work close to nature, and many times, you do not have to prove who you are or provide IDs.

- If you have any interest in antiques, consider buying space at weekend flea markets and selling your finds. The cost is often low. If you have an interest in some type of collecting, this is an ideal way to earn money while remaining invisible.

- Sell used books. Buy your books in quantity and resell them for a profit either online or at a flea market. You can do this anonymously over the Internet.

- Start peddling papers. Though not necessarily a high paying job, it is possible to make a living doing this. You may be able to work in this industry as an independent contractor.

Operate a Home Business

If you prefer to run your own business, and want to do it without registering with the government and possibly giving yourself away, be aware that it can get you into trouble. Operating a business without going through the proper government channels may go unnoticed, but remember, as said before, it is illegal to make money over a certain amount in the United States and not report it to the IRS. Problems for owners of unregistered home businesses frequently come from competitors or nosy neighbors. Do not tell your neighbors if you are working out of your home, and do not bring customers or clients to your home. Doing so is likely to bring about unwanted attention to your business.

There are all kinds of businesses to operate from home. The best businesses to maintain obscurity are operated using mail, phone, e-mail, and the Internet. Due to the ubiquity of the Internet, you can run a business of your own home without a physical identity. You do not have to see people in person and may not even need to speak with people over the phone. There is nothing illegal or suspicious about operating a business in this way, as it is the nature of the Internet. You can sell goods through sites such as Amazon.com or eBay and have your customers see nothing more than a username. You should be able to run a business of this type, or something else that meets your interests, while remaining as anonymous as your customers.

One issue to resolve, of course, is that most people take on businesses that reflect their own interests and work experience. You should be aware that your occupation can give your identity away to someone intent on locating you. You should also keep in mind that starting a business is risky under any conditions, but certainly more so for you because of your new identity. New businesses often fail within the first two years of opening, especially if certain aspects are neglected or forgotten. Make sure to research how to market yourself and effectively handle your finances. Also, establish a business plan for the future. Many people underestimate the importance of the last step. There are also insurance issues to be considered. For example, if you run a lawn care business, the vehicles must be insured, which can present a problem if you are trying to remain anonymous.

Another option for generating an income is affiliate marketing, a marketing practice in which a business rewards affiliates for each customer who visits a Web site brought about by the affiliate's marketing efforts. Users are usually paid cash or gifts for the referral of others to the site. Even if you have limited Internet skills, you might consider this type of work. You can find out more about affiliate marketing and how to start generating an income through affiliate marketing by visiting related Web sites or reading books on the topic.

Finding Work as an Expat

If choosing to live overseas, you can also find work, though it may be more complicated, as work permits vary from country to country. In addition, many third world or emerging countries are in dire need of people with technical, teaching, and sales skills. Computer operators are in demand everywhere. In today's technical world, fixing appliances is a valuable skill around the globe. Most countries also have a big demand for English teachers. However, in some countries you may be at a disadvantage because many employers prefer to hire fellow citizens first. This may be discrimination or it could be an actual legal requirement. This is especially true if unemployment rates are high. If this is the case, you may be ineligible for a job in that country, so you should research this before picking your destination. Not only do job demands vary from country to country, but regulations and conditions of employment also vary.

Because it is safe to speculate that most missing people have to work, the likelihood is that you will be job hunting. Whether your background is in theatre, accounting, or any number of other professions, there are Internet sites geared toward helping you find work. The following are a small sample of the many prominent Internet sites that can help establish employment, many of which also provide useful information about different countries:

- EscapeArtist.com (**www.escapeartist.com**) offers a section on "Jobs Overseas," which takes you to the "Jobs Overseas Index Page." The site also offers information on living overseas and listings of expatriate groups in various countries, plus a wide range of other resources for anyone who wants to start a new life overseas, such as currency conversions.

- TipTopJob.com (**www.tiptopjob.com**) is an international job search site that is free for those seeking a job in any field, but employers must pay to post.

- The European Council of International Schools (**www.esic.org**) offers education-related positions.

- The International Jobs Center (**http://internationaljobs.org**) has a "hot jobs" section that is updated daily. It costs $26 for a six-week subscription (six issues).

- Expatnetwork (**www.expatnetwork.com**) has a heavy emphasis on the oil, gas, construction, and agriculture industries worldwide. Job seekers can submit their résumés, but there is a charge, depending on the level of service.

- Transitions Abroad (**www.transitionsabroad.com**) has wide-ranging jobs that span the spectrum from teaching English in Japan to milking cows in Iceland.

Finding work in the country of your choice is similar to finding work in the United States. The following list details ten helpful tips for finding a job once you relocate to your new home:

1. Read the newspapers. Employers do still use them. Weekends are the best time for ads. In most countries, you are not expected to wait for a reply. Contact the employers politely.

2. Notice bulletin boards. These are all over in small villages and towns. You will find them in Internet cafés and restaurants, for example.

3. Look for local magazines that sometimes list jobs.

4. The tourist industry is often a good source of employment. Check out any publications distributed to tourists and/or visitors.

5. Employment agencies are not necessarily the best places to find employment if you wish to remain anonymous, but you might try them out. You may find, however, that you will have better luck contacting employers directly.

6. Check company Web sites. Many companies put openings on their sites.

7. Do some research into what the job market is like in the country you are thinking of moving to. That may help steer you toward jobs. In Costa Rica, for example, there is a growing eco-tourism movement. You could check out that segment of the tourism industry for available jobs.

8. Your résumé is always important. Make sure it looks professional and is free of spelling errors.

9. Organize yourself. Keep track of everything you do related to job searching. Use a simple spreadsheet to jot down information you collect during the process, such as employer contact information, jobs you have applied for, or dates and times for interviews.

10. Do not forget to send follow-up letters to employers within a few days of interviewing. These may be handwritten on a small card with a brief message.

Better your chances of landing a job

One of the first things you should realize is that a résumé geared toward employment in the United States most likely is not adequate for gaining employment outside the United States. Research how to write a curriculum vita, which is a more detailed document noting your education and work experience. This may be difficult for you as someone who wishes to remain anonymous, but resist the temptation to lie. There is no reason a company would recognize you as your old identity if you have a new legal name.

An easy booster to your credentials is to formally train to teach English for speakers of other languages (ESOL) courses. Fluency in your new country's native language is also an obvious necessity, so take language courses or attempt to pick up the language as you go about your daily life. Many countries hire foreign workers who possess certain skills, so research various countries you are interested in moving to and see what type of jobs they are looking to fill. You will need to acquire a work permit, but in many countries, the company that wants to hire you must sponsor you, so you are not the one who completes this paperwork. You should also research the work permit laws of the country you wish to move to, as all are not easily renewable. You may even have to leave a country quickly if you lose your job.

Misinformation about laws in foreign countries is common, so it is in your best interest to speak to a lawyer who knows about immigration laws. Contacting immigration services in another country can, obviously, be time consuming and confusing, but this is an option; although, speaking to a professional before you leave the Untied State will likely provide better results.

The legal documentation of working in a foreign country

Each country has different laws and requirements about who can work in the country and for how long. Foreigners who come to work in a new country may be legally required to have a work permit to hold a job in that country. Most countries do all they can to preserve jobs for citizens, but some countries do not have enough citizens who are skilled in certain trades, so they offer permits to foreigners to fill these jobs. To qualify, you usually must have extensive experience and a college degree. However, just having a work permit does not grant entry into the country. Some countries have good relations with each other and do not require visas for foreign visitors from those countries, but a visa might still be necessary. Obviously, if you have assumed a new identity, acquiring a visa or other travel document may prove to be difficult.

Basically, it boils down to what country you are coming from and why you are traveling to the country. These two pieces of information dictate what documentation is needed. Obviously, countries want to make it as easy as possible for travelers to visit because of money made through tourism, whereas someone looking for work is potentially taking money out of the that country. Every country wants to better itself, so you will only be welcomed as a worker if you benefit the country.

Always try to start your research with the official government Web site that has current information regarding immigration. Many unofficial sites often try to charge for forms that you can obtain for free or have outdated information listed. Because work laws are numerous and varied, the upcoming example explains what is needed in order to legally work in the United Kingdom. This will give you an idea of the information necessary to research and show you how long it commonly takes to complete this process.

The United Kingdom's Border Agency Web site can be found at **www.ukba.homeoffice.gov.uk**. The United Kingdom has a point-based system with five tiers that divide potential immigrants into categories. First, you would need to find out which category you fall under. Then, you must earn a certain number of points under that tier's point-based "test" to be hired. The test is really a questionnaire that reflects how beneficial you are to the needs of the United Kingdom.

The point-based system was launched on February 29, 2008. Basically, a potential immigrant earns points for skills, previous salary, experience, and age. The point system is flexible in that it changes with the demand of a given job market. There are many different acceptable professions and jobs that qualify someone to work in the United Kingdom, so they have divided them into tiers and adjusted the points test for each tier. The United Kingdom Border Agency divides the tiers and sub categories as such:

- *Tier 1* – Highly skilled individuals
  - **General:** For people who are looking for highly skilled employment in the United Kingdom, or are self-employed or setting up a business.
  - **Investor:** For people who are making a large investment in the United Kingdom.

  - **Entrepreneur:** For people who are investing in the United Kingdom by setting up or taking over the running of a business.
  - **Post-study work:** For people who are studying now or have studied in the past in the United Kingdom.

- *Tier* 2 — Skilled workers with a job offer
  - **General:** For skilled workers who have a job offer from a licensed sponsor and are coming to fill a gap in the workforce that cannot be filled by a settled worker.
  - **Intra-company transfer:** For employees of multinational companies who are being transferred by their overseas employer to a skilled job in a United Kingdom-based branch of the organization.
  - **Minister of religion:** For people coming to the United Kingdom as religious workers within religious organizations for more than two years.
  - **Sportsperson:** For elite sportspeople and coaches who are internationally established at the highest level and will make a significant contribution to the development of their sport.

- *Tier 3* — For limited numbers of low-skilled workers needed to fill temporary labor shortages
  - This tier is suspended indefinitely, but in theory could arise again should the need become apparent.

- *Tier 4* — Students
  - **Adult student (also known as general student):** For people coming to the United Kingdom for their post-16 education.
  - **Child student:** For children between 4 and 17 years old who are coming to the United Kingdom for their education. Those between 4 and 15 years old may only be educated at independent fee-paying schools.
- *Tier 5* — Temporary workers and young people covered by the Youth Mobility Scheme
  - **Temporary worker — creative and sporting:** For people coming to the United Kingdom to work or perform as sportspeople, entertainers, or creative artists for up to 12 months.
  - **Temporary worker — charity workers:** For people coming to the United Kingdom to do voluntary (unpaid) work for charity.
  - **Temporary worker — religious workers:** For people coming to the United Kingdom to work temporarily as a religious worker.
  - **Temporary worker — government authorized exchange:** For people coming to the United Kingdom through approved schemes that aim to share knowledge, experience, and best practice, while experiencing the social and cultural life of the United Kingdom.

- **Temporary worker — international agreement:** For people coming to the United Kingdom under contract to do work that is covered under international law. This includes the General Agreement on Trade in Services (GATS), similar agreements between the United Kingdom and another country, employees of overseas governments and international organizations, and private servants in diplomatic households
- **Youth Mobility Scheme:** For young people from participating countries who would like to experience life in the United Kingdom

Most likely, you will need a job offer from a sponsor to qualify for a work permit. Those who apply under tier two or five must supply a certificate of sponsorship from a licensed sponsor. The only tier that does not require a sponsor is tier one, and this is to encourage the investors and entrepreneurs to add to the United Kingdom's economy. The tiers are interchangeable, meaning if you would like to switch from tier two to tier one, and you qualify, you may. This helps some stay in the United Kingdom longer. The only tier you cannot switch out of is tier five. You must go back to your country and reapply to come back to the United Kingdom under a different tier.

Everyone applying to enter the United Kingdom through this system must also have maintenance funds in the equivalent of 2,800 pounds (about $4,250). This money must be present in your bank account for at least the three months before you apply and must never dip below 2,800 pounds during that time. Joint accounts can be used to qualify as well. This is your insurance, and no matter what happens with your job in the United Kingdom, you will be able to support yourself for some time without money from the government. Because you are not a U.K. citizen, you would not be eligible for public funds and could essentially become trapped in the United Kingdom if no one could send you money. As someone who has disappeared, this is something to consider.

Once an application is accepted, there is even more to work on, such as making sure paperwork stays up to date with information regarding things like visa expiration periods. As you can see, this process is pretty exhaustive, and you will need a lot of time to legally get a job in other countries. As someone who is looking to hide sooner rather than later, this may be another good reason to hide in the United States first, before becoming an expatriate.

chapter 8

Money Issues as an Expat

If you want to run away to another country but keep American citizenship, you still have to file American taxes. You will need to learn about the "foreign-earned-income exclusion." This permits U.S. citizens and resident aliens to exclude more than $80,000 of the income they earn while living outside the United States, if they meet certain qualifications.

How to Quality for Exclusions

You can hire a lawyer to research your individual case, but the IRS explains how you qualify on its Web site. In essence, by meeting certain requirements, you may qualify for the foreign-earned-income exclusion, foreign-housing exclusion, and the foreign-housing deduction. If you are a U.S. citizen or resident alien of the United States and you live abroad, you are taxed on your worldwide income. Yet, you may qualify to exclude from income up to $85,700 of your foreign earnings. In addition, it is possible to exclude or deduct certain foreign housing amounts.

You may also be entitled to exclude from income the value of meals and lodging provided to you by your employer. To claim the foreign-earned-income exclusion, the foreign-housing exclusion, or the foreign-housing deduction, you must meet all three of the following requirements:

1. Your tax home must be in a foreign country.
2. You must have foreign-earned income.
3. You must be either:

    a. A U.S. citizen who is a bona fide resident of a foreign country or countries for an uninterrupted period that includes an entire tax year,

    b. A U.S. resident alien who is a citizen or national of a country with which the United States has an income-tax treaty in effect and who is a bona fide resident of a foreign country or countries for an uninterrupted period that includes an entire tax year, or

    c. A U.S. citizen or resident alien who is physically present in a foreign country or countries for at least 330 full days during any period of 12 consecutive months.

The minimum time requirements for bona fide residence and physical presence can be waived if you must leave a foreign country because of war, civil unrest, or similar adverse conditions in that country.

To qualify for the foreign-earned-income exclusion, the foreign-housing exclusion, or the foreign-housing deduction, your tax home must be in a foreign country throughout your period of bona fide residence or physical presence abroad.

Where is Your Tax Home?

Your tax home is the broad area of your main place of business, employment, or post of duty, regardless of where you maintain your family home. Your tax home is the place where you are permanently or indefinitely engaged to work as an employee or self-employed individual. Having a tax home in a given location does not necessarily mean that the given location is your residence or domicile for tax purposes.

If you do not have a regular or main place of business because of the nature of your work, your tax home may be the place where you regularly live. If you have neither a regular nor main place of business, nor a place where you regularly live, you are considered an itinerant, and your tax home is wherever you work.

You are not considered to have a tax home in a foreign country for any period in which your abode is in the United States. Though, your abode is not necessarily in the United States while you are temporarily in the United States. Your abode is also not necessarily in the United States merely because you maintain a dwelling in the United States, regardless of whether your spouse or dependents use the dwelling.

Abode has been variously defined as one's home, habitation, residence, domicile, or place of dwelling. It does not mean your principal place of business. Abode has a domestic rather than a vocational meaning, and does not mean the same as tax home. The location of your abode often will depend on where you maintain your economic, family, and personal ties.

For example, if you happen to be employed on an offshore oil rig in the territorial waters of a foreign country and work a 28-day on/28-day off schedule, and you return to your family residence in the United States during your off periods, you are considered to have an abode in the United States. This does not satisfy the tax home test in the foreign country. You cannot claim either of the exclusions or the housing deduction.

Suppose, on the other hand, that for several years, you were a marketing executive with a producer of machine tools in Toledo, Ohio. In November of last year, your employer transferred you to London, England, for a minimum of 18 months to set up a sales operation for Europe. Before you left, you distributed business cards showing your business and home addresses in London. You kept ownership of your home in Toledo, but rented it to another family and placed your car in storage. In November of last year, you moved your spouse, children, furniture, and family pets to a home your employer rented for you in London.

Shortly after moving, say you leased a car and you and your spouse got British driver's licenses. Your entire family got library cards for the local public library. You and your spouse opened bank accounts with a London bank and secured consumer credit. You joined a local business league and both you and your spouse became active in the neighborhood civic association and also worked with a local charity. Your abode is in London for the time you live there. You satisfy the tax home test in the foreign country.

The location of your tax home often depends on whether your assignment is temporary or indefinite. If you are temporarily absent from your tax home in the United States on business, you may be able to deduct your away-from-home expenses, such as travel, meals, and lodging, but you would not qualify for the foreign-earned-income exclusion.

If your new work assignment is for an indefinite period, your new place of employment becomes your tax home, and you would not be able to deduct any related expenses that you have in the broad area of this new work assignment. If your new tax home is in a foreign country, and you meet the other requirements, your earnings may qualify for the foreign-earned-income exclusion.

If you expect your employment away from home in a single location to last for a year or less, and it does, it is temporary unless facts and circumstances indicate otherwise. If you expect it to last for more than a year, it is indefinite. If you expect it to last for a year or less, but at some later date you then expect it to last longer than a year, it is temporary, in the absence of facts and circumstances indicating otherwise, until your expectation changes.

To meet the bona fide residence or physical presence tests, you must live in or be present in a foreign country. A foreign country frequently is any territory, including the air space and territorial waters, under the sovereignty of a government other than that of the United States.

The term "foreign country" includes the seabed and subsoil of those submarine areas adjacent to the territorial waters of a foreign country and over which the foreign country has exclusive rights under international law to explore and exploit the natural resources.

Living in American Territories

The term "foreign country" does not include Puerto Rico, Guam, the Commonwealth of the Northern Mariana Islands, the U.S. Virgin Islands, or U.S. possessions, such as Johnston Island because they are American territories. For purposes of the foreign-earned-income exclusion, the foreign-housing exclusion, and the foreign-housing deduction, the terms "foreign," "abroad," and "overseas" refer to areas outside the United States, American Samoa, Guam, the Commonwealth of the Northern Mariana Islands, Puerto Rico, the U.S. Virgin Islands, and the Antarctic region.

Residence or presence in a U.S. possession does not qualify you for the foreign-earned-income exclusion. You may, however, qualify for an exclusion of your possession income on your U.S. return.

There is a possession exclusion available to individuals who are bona fide residents of American Samoa for the entire tax year. Gross income from sources within American Samoa may be eligible for this exclusion. Income that is effectively connected with the conduct of a trade or business within American Samoa also may be eligible.

Residents of Puerto Rico and the U.S. Virgin Islands cannot claim the foreign-earned-income or foreign-housing exclusions.

Normally, if you are a U.S. citizen who is a bona fide resident of Puerto Rico for the entire tax year, you are not subject to U.S. taxes on income from Puerto Rican sources. This does not include amounts paid for services performed as an employee of the United States. Yet, you are subject to U.S. tax on your income from sources outside Puerto Rico. In figuring your U.S. tax, you cannot deduct expenses allocable to income not subject to tax.

You meet the bona fide residence test if you are a resident of a foreign country or countries for an uninterrupted period, including an entire tax year. You can use the bona fide residence test to qualify for the exclusions and the deduction only if you are either:

- A U.S. citizen, or
- A U.S. resident alien who is a citizen or national of a country with which the United States has an income tax treaty in effect.

You do not automatically acquire bona fide resident status merely by living in a foreign country or countries for one year. If you go to a foreign country to work on a particular job for a specified period of time, you ordinarily will not be regarded as a bona fide resident of that country, even though you work there for one tax year or longer. The length of your stay and the nature of your job are only two of the factors to be considered in determining whether you meet the bona fide residence test.

To meet the bona fide residence test, you must have established such a residence in a foreign country. Your bona fide residence is not necessarily the same as your domicile. Your domicile is your permanent home, the place to which you always return or intend to return. You could have your domicile in Cleveland, Ohio, and a bona fide residence in Edinburgh, Scotland, if you intend to return eventually to Cleveland. The fact that you go to Scotland does not automatically make Scotland your bona fide residence.

If you go there as a tourist or on a short business trip, and return to the United States, you have not established bona fide residence in Scotland. However, if you go to Scotland to work for an indefinite or extended period, and set up permanent quarters there for yourself and your family, you most likely have established a bona fide residence in a foreign country, even though you intend to return eventually to the United States. You are clearly not a resident of Scotland in the first instance. Yet, in the second, you are a resident because your stay in Scotland appears to be permanent. If your residency is not as clearly defined as either of these illustrations, it may be more difficult to decide whether you have established a bona fide residence.

Bona Fide Residency Guidelines

Questions of bona fide residence are determined according to each individual case, taking into account factors such as your intention, the purpose of your trip, and the nature and length of your stay abroad.

You must show the IRS that you have been a bona fide resident of a foreign country or countries for an uninterrupted period that includes an entire tax year. An entire tax year is from January 1 through December 31 for taxpayers who file their income tax returns on a calendar-year basis. The IRS decides whether you are a bona fide resident of a foreign country largely based on facts you report.

An income tax exemption provided in a treaty or other international agreement will not in itself prevent you from being a bona fide resident of a foreign country. Whether a treaty prevents you from becoming a bona fide resident of a foreign country is determined under all provisions of the treaty, including specific provisions relating to residence or privileges and immunities.

If you are a U.S. citizen living abroad, you can vote by absentee ballot in any election held in the United States without risking your status as a bona fide resident of a foreign country.

However, if you give information to the local election officials about the nature and length of your stay abroad that does not match the information you give for the bona fide residence test, the information given in connection with absentee voting will be considered in determining your status, but will not necessarily be conclusive.

Meeting the bona fide residence test

During the period of bona fide residence in a foreign country, you can leave the country for brief or temporary trips back to the United States or elsewhere for vacation or business. To keep your status as a bona fide resident of a foreign country, you must have a clear intention of returning from such trips without unreasonable delay to your foreign residence or a new bona fide residence in another foreign country.

There is also a physical presence test. To pass the physical presence test, you must be physically present in a foreign country, or countries, 330 full days during a period of 12 consecutive months. The 330 days do not have to be consecutive. Any U.S. citizen or resident alien can use the physical presence test to qualify for the exclusions and deductions.

The physical presence test is based only on how long you stay in a foreign country or countries. This test does not depend on the kind of residence you establish, your intentions about returning, or the nature and purpose of your stay abroad. You can count days you spent abroad for any reason. You do not have to be in a foreign country only for employment purposes it can include vacation time. You do not meet the physical presence test if illness, family problems, a vacation, or your employer's orders cause you to be present for less than the required amount of time.

There are exceptions. You can be physically present in a foreign country or countries for less than 330 full days and still meet the physical presence test if you are required to leave a country because of war or civil unrest, for example.

If, in traveling from the United States to a foreign country, you pass over a foreign country before midnight of the day you leave, the first day you can count toward the 330-day total is the day following the day you leave the United States. For example, of you leave the United States for France by air on June 10 and arrive in France at 9 a.m. on June 11, your first full day of physical presence in France is June 12.

If you leave the United States by air at 9:30 a.m. on June 10 to travel to Kenya and pass over western Africa at 11 p.m. on June 10 and arrive in Kenya at 12:30 a.m. on June 11, then your first full day in a foreign country is June 11.

You can move about from one place to another in a foreign country or to another foreign country without losing full days. If any part of your travel is not within any foreign country but takes less than 24 hours, you are considered to be in a foreign country during that part of travel.

There are four rules you should know when figuring the 12-month period:

- Your 12-month period can begin with any day of the month. It ends the day before the same calendar day, 12 months later.

- Your 12-month period must be made up of consecutive months. Any 12-month period can be used if the 330 days in a foreign country fall within that period.

- You do not have to begin your 12-month period with your first full day in a foreign country or end it with the day you leave. You can choose the 12-month period that gives you the most exclusion.

- In determining whether the 12-month period falls within a longer stay in the foreign country, 12-month periods can overlap one another.

The IRS uses this example of calculating your foreign-source earned income:

You are a U.S. citizen, a bona fide resident of Canada, and working as a mining engineer. Your salary is $76,800 per year. You also receive a $6,000 cost of living allowance, and a $6,000 education allowance. Your employment contract did not indicate that you were entitled to these allowances only while outside the United States. Your total income is $88,800. You work a five-day week, Monday through Friday. After subtracting your vacation, you have a total of 240 workdays in the year. You worked in the United States during the year for six weeks (30 workdays). The following shows how to figure the part of your income that is for work done in the United State during the year.

Number of days worked in the U.S. during the year	(30)	**× Total income ($88,800) = $11,100**
Number of days of work during the year for which payment was made	(240)	

Your U.S. source-earned income is $11,100.

Source: Internal Revenue Service's Tax Guide for U.S. Citizens and Resident Aliens Abroad

chapter 9

Keeping Your New Identity Safe

Disappearing is the easy part. Staying hidden takes much more work and is a way of life. Guarding your privacy can mean limiting options when it comes to products, services, and living arrangements. This is why it is so important to change your name before you settle down. If you do something like purchase a house in your old name, the mortgage and deed are under that name and are public record. So even if you change your name at a later time, if you still live in that house or have a connection to it you may be found.

In this technology driven world, anyone who is looking for you has a number of resources available, and many of them are low cost or free. Always be frugal about dispersing contact information, and unless it is absolutely necessary, do not give it out to any person or company. Places like your bank have more strict privacy policies regarding your information than social networking sites or online stores.

There are many ways professionals and even amateurs can track down your location, and this will be discussed more thoroughly in the next chapter. The best way to stop anyone from succeeding is to plan your disappearance from the beginning, and pay attention to details. You may feel like you are being overly paranoid, but if you truly want to disappear, you need to step in the shoes of those who will be looking for you and get rid of all their resources before they have a chance to use them.

One of your goals is to throw off anyone trying to follow you. You can get a phone number in any state or almost any country from various providers. When someone calls your number, with a personalized recording, you can have your message forwarded to your e-mail address. That way, you can retrieve your messages from anywhere in the world. No one can tell where you are because your whereabouts cannot be traced through your phone or e-mail address.

Be sure to pay for your account for a year or more so it does not show up on your credit card statement in coming months. Investigators trying to get your address will only have an untraceable e-mail. Furthermore, do not do your searching from your home or work computers. Go to an Internet café and do all research there. Leave no tracks where private investigators may go, such as your home or office computer.

There are a huge number of resources, which have data from you that might be used for locating you. These include:

- The telephone company
- Your cell phone

- Your pager
- Your internet provider
- Cable TV
- Credit cards
- Library card
- Discount cards
- Airlines
- Groups and associations
- Magazine subscriptions
- Newspaper subscriptions
- Utility companies

The Internet

The Internet has become such an ingrained part of the day-to-day lives of most people that you will likely find it hard to keep information private. Before leaving, you should have deleted every online account possible, especially ones on social networking sites. Do not make a profile using your new identity even if you never intend to upload photos or even make your account public. It is amazing how much information "friends of friends" can see, and you never know who could recognize a photo your new best friend uploaded and "tagged" to your profile.

You may also have to worry about facial recognition tools that identify people by certain distinct facial features. Although this technology is still being improved and it is not quite mainstream, it has been a topic of serious interest since Sept. 11 as a method of identifying known terrorists. L-1 Identity Solutions is a leader in the industry and works with police departments and the governments of 20 countries including the United States. It was formerly known as Viisage Technology, the company in charge of the unannounced biometrics surveillance at Super Bowl XXXV in Tampa Bay, Fla., which identified 19 criminals in attendance of the game. Every guest who entered the stadium has his or her picture taken discreetly, which was then compared to the police database of mug shots.

Although you may never have been arrested, this technology is also used by the Center for Missing and Exploited Children to compare a family photo against photographs on the Internet. It is easy to see how this technology could spread to include everyone and be used for countless applications, such as finding a missing person. Any time you visit an ATM, bank, mall, or airport, you are photographed, and the photo could be added to a database. If the police have a reason to believe you are in danger and not a voluntary missing person, this technology could be applied to your search. The United Kingdom already uses biometrics quite vastly and even requires entrance into the system to get a visa. The United Kingdom Border Agency Web site says, "To protect the integrity of the visa system and to protect our customers, we require every United Kingdom Border Agency visa applicant around the world to enroll their fingerprints, and to have a digital photograph taken when they make a visa application."

Hopefully, the people looking for you are only relying on their eyes to identify you. If this is the case, you could hire Reputation Defender (**www.reputationdefender.com**) to eliminate as much of your data as possible from the Internet. If you were very social and built up large Internet presence this is a great option for you.

This service should be used right as you were leaving, because if they found a missing persons report, they may report you.

Internet security

Some basic steps for securing information on your computer were discussed in Chapter 2, but there are some new steps you should take once you are in your new life. Do not use any computer to access personal information that is not owned by you. There is no way to tell what software is installed on someone else's computer unless you inspect it thoroughly and they have anti-virus software. Their computer could also automatically store information in the browser history, cookies, and search engine entries. There are also programs that record keystrokes and monitor all Internet activity that are commonly used by businesses to monitor employee computer activity. This means managers and others who have access to the programs can see not only the Web sites you visit, but the username and passwords you type in. You should not use office computers for your personal ventures anyway, but sometimes you are allowed to if you are off the clock. Do not do this, as you never know when all that collected information could be used against you.

The Privacy Rights Clearinghouse discusses business-monitoring rights at **www.privacyrights.org/fs/fs7-work.htm**. Though many companies do inform employees of their monitoring habits, there is no law that says they must inform you.

Search engines, such as Google, Yahoo, and MSN, all collect data from your searches and store it for a certain amount of time. This includes recording a computer's IP address and then listing each web page that IP address views. Regardless of what search engine or Web browser you use, you need to read its privacy policy and see what happens to your information as well as what settings you have control over. Ixquick (**www.ixquick.com**) does not store any user data.

Be sure to have security software on your computer. While many of the major name brands are very effective, they are also costly. Instead, visit CNET's Web site (**http://download.cnet.com**) or thefreecountry.com (**www.thefreecountry.com**) to download antivirus software. These sites are extremely safe and check all of the offered software for any viruses. While there, you should also look into free firewall programs.

Firewalls stop the free flow of data from entering and leaving your computer. You must configure your firewall to allow the safe information and block the rest. Many people dislike firewalls because they often block information the user wants, but it is easy to change the settings to allow individual Web sites and programs to function.

It is a good practice never to store your password in your wallet, purse, or on a sticky note on your monitor. You should also be extremely careful about password-hint options at web sites. Make sure the hint is not a giveaway to someone who knows a little about you, such as your favorite pet or your wife's name.

Computer forensic experts use password-cracking programs that can essentially pull up any real words in any language. That obviously means it would be best not to use a common phrase or real word password. One useful suggestion is to take the first letter of each word in a familiar phase. For example, the phrase "early to bed and early to rise" would be "ETBAETR." Then add numbers or other special characters and upper and lower case letters as well. The more diverse, the better.

Some common names for passwords should also be avoided, including:

- Administrator
- Mypass
- Love
- Login
- Owner
- Home
- Internet
- Computer
- Enable
- Password

The type of computer you use is also important and a laptop is the best way to preserve your privacy. With a laptop, you can use removable storage units that can be taken out when it is not in use. Do not neglect to store them in a safe place, preferably a locked safe. When traveling, you can slip your storage into your pocket or leave it behind. Another advantage to using a laptop is that it is easy to hide. If you do not have a safe, you can create a small space to safely hide your laptop in your home.

Despite all of this, one of the key advantages of the Internet for someone in hiding is its virtual life. In the past, for those who wanted to disappear, it was necessary to create an entire new identity, but with the Internet, you can use its tools to live and work without being found. You can obtain pay-as-you-go cell phones and prepaid credit cards. It is also relatively simple to run a business from a Web site with no brick-and-mortar addresses, which is a key element when people are trying to find you.

Visit these Web sites for more information on Internet security:

- The Center for Democracy and Technology (**www.cdt.org/privacy/guide**) offers a free online guide to online privacy.
- The Electronic Privacy Information Center (**www.epic.org**) includes much more than just Internet security, but also any information relevant to your First Amendment and constitutional rights.

Ways to protect your Internet privacy

Here are ten ways to help protect your privacy on the Internet:

1. Read privacy policies. Although this is not the most fun thing to do, you are a person in hiding and need to know what is going on with your information. Once you get in the habit of reading and understanding privacy policies, it will become second nature.

2. Update all your security software. All anti-virus and anti-malware programs need to be updated as often as possible because thieves and hackers are constantly coming up with new programs and codes that can harm your computer.

3. Never open unsolicited e-mails. Even though many are harmless, it is usually junk mail anyway. If you need a product, you can research it yourself and do not need to rely on advertisements to tell you what to buy.

4. Do not click on unknown links. This includes online and in your e-mails. It is extremely common and easy for programs to be embedded in links and downloaded to your computer without your knowledge.

5. Learn what ads look like. Although some advertisements are obvious, many others blend in with the contents of the Web page. Just because a Web site is legitimate, it does not mean the ads are legitimate, as many sites have little or no control over which ads appear on their page.

6. Do not download "freebies". There are countless free games, wallpapers, toolbars, and screen savers available online. Unless you know for a fact it is safe, do not download it. There are often hidden spyware programs, or worse things, attached to these downloads that can corrupt your computer and collect your data. Even well-known toolbars are best avoided.

7. Do not illegally download anything. While there are many sites that allow you to download movies, music, and even software, these sites are laden with malware and spyware. Besides, they are illegal. Your ISP may even cancel your service or report to FBI if you commit illegal downloads.

8. Be wary of using free Wi-Fi. If you can connect to a wireless Internet connection, such as those offered in cafes and

hotels, without any password or other security measures, the data you transmit can be visible to others who have the right software. It is best to use your own Internet service for viewing sensitive sites, such as your online banking or bill paying.

9. Do not use social networking sites. Even if you implement all of the privacy features on a social networking site, the nature of these sites is against everything you are trying to accomplish as a person who has vanished. The police and private investigators have successfully tracked down many people through social networking sites.

10. Do not visit sites with adult content. Although some of these are secure, they are costly and require you to register with a credit card. The free ones are often filled with malware and spyware.

There is no foolproof way to send e-mail or contact anyone through the Internet. Messages may linger for years in an inbox and, therefore, could reappear in your life at any time. The best way to communicate while in hiding is the old-fashioned way. Seal a letter in an envelope, stamp it, and mail it. That is simply the safest way to communicate if you want to be sure no one is looking into your personal communications.

CASE STUDY: WANTED FUGITIVES AND BLOGGING

"A Japanese man wanted on murder charges for 25 years was arrested because of a blog. The man was believed to have killed his wife while visiting the United States in 1981. He was tried and convicted in Japan, but the case was overturned. He was on the loose in Japan, where he started blogging. U.S. police officials monitored his blog to see if he would be foolish enough to announce travel to a U.S. territory where they had jurisdiction — which he finally did. He was quickly arrested."

Source: Techdirt.com
Used with Permission

Telephone

Experts on privacy invariably agree telephones are insecure by nature. Believe it or not, private investigators routinely find people by calling the local directory system. Investigators say people have come into their offices willing to spend hundreds or even thousands of dollars to find someone who is listed in the White Pages. This should not happen to you if you followed the advice in this book. For example, many have forsaken landline phones in favor of cell phones because there really is no need to have both. Instead of a cell phone with a plan, buy a prepaid cell phone. The per-minute cost is high, but it is the best choice because it avoids deposits, contracts, credit checks, minimum monthly fees, and there is no identification required. Furthermore, there is no request for a social security number. Some of these phones are disposable, and that is something you want to consider because you will regularly throw away your phone to get a different number.

If you feel you must have a landline phone, follow these tips to help hide your identity:

- Do not rely on an unlisted telephone number in the hope it will offer some anonymity. Unlisted telephone numbers now appear routinely on the Internet, as well in directories and reserves searches.

- Avoid calling toll-free numbers. All of these have automatic number identifications. These numbers eventually end up in various databases available to private investigators. The numbers may even end up in data available to the public.

- Disguise your name in telephone records, perhaps by using a middle name or initial and last name.

It is not always the most convenient option, but the best way to keep telephone conversations private is by using a pay phone. To truly protect your privacy, you would need to regularly use a different phone.

The simplest answer is to use a standard, digital corded telephone, which is preferable to cordless or wireless phones. Although the convenience of a cordless phone is obvious, they are very insecure. Their signals are easy to pick up with simple devices, such as baby monitors, because cordless phones transmit a signal from the handheld piece to the base piece, much like a radio does. Anyone who finds the station can "tune in." Cordless phone signals can also get mixed, and if your neighbor has one as well, he or she might be able to hear your calls accidentally. Radio scanners can also pick up cordless phone calls. Whether the person using the scanner is a police officer, private investigator, or a paranoid neighbor, you do not want people listening in on your calls.

Caller ID

Almost all phones come equipped with caller ID, which shows where the call is coming from. As someone who is trying to minimize the spread of personal contact information, you should block your number from appearing on caller IDs. If you have a regular landline or cell phone, simply call the provider and ask about caller ID blocking services. You can block your line entirely, which is not the best idea because many people do not answer blocked calls, or you can block your number for individual calls using the service code *67. Simply dial *67 and then the number you are calling, and your number will not appear on the caller ID. This service is free and works on landlines and cellular phones. The only exceptions are if you call the police, dial 911, or call a toll-free number because they can always see your phone number on their caller ID systems. Always test your phone before you call someone using *67, just to be safe.

Avoid using this service to call loved ones. If they were determined and knowledgeable, they could dial *57 right after your call. This reports your call as harassing or obscene to the telephone company, who then turns your number over to the authorities. While this does not give the person direct access to your number, they may be able to contact the police to find you because you are a missing person.

Another option you can use for occasional blocking is the services of Caller ID Faker (**www.calleridfaker.com**). This company allows you to display a fake number on caller IDs in place of your real number. It also allows you to change the sound of your voice and record the phone call. You can pay a monthly fee for unlimited use, or buy a certain number of uses for a set price. You can make calls for free, but they are limited to two minutes.

Cell phone security

Cell phones with special features might be tempting, but as a person in hiding, you need to consider how unsecure these devices are. Smart phones could easily be called "spy phones" because someone with the right tools can access anything you do with your phone, store on your phone, and even your location. If you have one of these phones and are planning to leave in the near future, get rid of it immediately. All someone needs to know is your phone number and they can find you very quickly, as many cell phone companies will gladly send them your call records and even activate your phone's GPS to find your exact location. They might not even need to go through the police to access this information, but if they did, the police would likely provide them with help. Often just faxing a copy of the missing persons report is enough.

Many businesspeople use smart phones for work. If you must have one for your job, be sure to never use it for anything personal. Smart phones back up data with your service provider's servers, which means the police can subpoena your records. Think of all the famous people who have gotten in trouble because of text messages, pictures, and e-mails on their phones. Many people who work for cell phone service providers are going to have access to your stored data. Keep in mind it is currently legal for your boss to remotely monitor your phone if he or she furnishes it to you through the company.

Smart phones are like tiny computers, but unfortunately, you cannot clean the hard drive as easily as you can with your desktop or laptop. Fragments of all your data will remain on your phone even if you delete them. You can go to **www.recellular.com/recycling/data_eraser/default.asp** and input your service provider and phone model to receive instructions on how to completely clear the phone of personal data. Additionally, because they are mini-computers, smart phones are susceptible to malware and spyware that could also compromise data.

There are also many programs people can use to track your location when you have your phone with you. Currently, they need to be installed on your phone, meaning someone else would have to be in possession of your phone for a brief amount of time. FlexiSPY (**www.flexispy.com**) is a program that can be installed on your phone that sends detailed spreadsheets of all your data to whoever installed it. As long as the phone accesses the Internet, which all smart phones do, this program can automatically relay your data. Additionally, there is no way for you to see the program on your phone either.

The best way to protect your cell phone is to call your service provider and tell it to put a password on your account, so no one can pretend to be you and request information, and to have the call details removed from your bill. The only disadvantage to the latter is you will have problems disputing any incorrect charges that could occur with your bill. You should also buy a basic cell phone that does not have Internet access and turn the phone off when not in use. This will immensely limit the potential insecurities of owning a cell phone.

Prepaid cell phones

Buying a prepaid, or "pay as you go," cell phone is an even better idea. You are not bound by any contracts, but instead buy "airtime," or individual minutes for a set price. These phones are easy to buy, simple to activate, and can be very difficult to trace. Purchase one from a store and pay in cash as using the Internet will require you to pay with a credit card, which is obviously traceable. If you want to get a new number, you can simply let the phone deactivate, which happens when you do not add enough minutes in a set amount of time. You could also just buy a new phone.

Most of the prepaid cell phone providers also use the equipment and services of other providers, which means personal information could be seen or captured by others outside of your provider. Tracfone, a popular company for prepaid cell phones, mentions this in their privacy policy, "When TRACFONE uses third parties to perform services on its behalf, TRACFONE will request that such third parties protect your customer identifiable information consistently with this privacy policy. However, we cannot ensure that all of your customer identifiable information will never be disclosed, as regulatory and/or other requirements may make disclosure necessary."

All cell phones work by bouncing signals off cell phone towers, which means your location is possible to triangulate even with a prepaid cell phone. Also, conspiracy theories aside, the FBI can remotely activate your cell phone and listen to the conversation in the room where the phone is located. The FBI did this to capture and incriminate members of the Genovese mafia family. While this should have nothing to do with you as a regular person who just wants to disappear, it serves as a reminder that you will get caught if you are involved in illegal activities.

Mail

Do not file for a change of address though the postal service. Anyone who sends you mail during the first year will receive a notification of your new address, and then after one year will simply receive the sent mail back with a yellow sticker informing them of your new address. Instead, you need to manually switch your address with each company that you cannot part ties with. Ideally, you will not have to do this at all because you will close your bank account and no longer need to pay the bills at your old residence.

Once you do have a new residence, regardless of whether it is a house, apartment, or even an extended stay hotel, you should request all bills be sent to you electronically. In an effort to reduce paper waste and be more "green," almost every company offers billing statements through the Internet rather than physical mail. This should basically eliminate your need to even get mail, at least for a while. At some point, you will likely need to order a product that must be shipped to you, or you will be situated in your new life and need mail services just to appear normal. Your new friends and possibly family members will start to wonder why you are so secretive and have no easy means of contacting you. You should get a post office box for all mail once this is the case, rather than have anything delivered to your home.

Some people who disappear obtain post office boxes to keep their physical location secret. Some go even further and find out whether their local post office has a video camera. If they see electronic surveillance, they often find a smaller post office or another place to have mail delivered. You might not go that far to protect your privacy, but mail and other types of communication are areas you need to consider.

Getting a post office box is a good idea, but you have to understand the difference between the public and private boxes you can rent. Public boxes are what you rent at the U.S. Post Office. Private are commercial mail-receiving agencies, such as Mail Boxes Etc., PostNet, and Business Centers. It is a good idea to rent a regular post office box for your personal mail and get a private mailbox for business mail, deliveries from FedEx, and other mail. FedEx and United Parcel Service, and possibly other services will not deliver to a U.S. postal box. This is why a private mailbox is a good idea.

The major reason for continuing concern over postal matters is to discourage anyone from finding you through your mail, but the post office box also lets you avoid giving out your street address. The best post office box is one as far away from your home as possible, but still convenient enough for you to pick up mail once or twice a week.

There are fewer risks and fewer requirements from private mail providers. It is almost certainly worth the risk of identifying yourself to get a public post office box, though you should be aware that there are drawbacks.

For total anonymity, along with a new name, some people have been known to "take over" a person's mailbox. Perhaps someone in your neighborhood is moving away and is in need of a cash contribution from someone who wants to buy his or her mailbox. You should always make sure to get permission from this person before doing so, as tampering with mail is a federal offense. If given permission to receive mail at this mailbox you can use this person's basic name, with slight alterations, as if it were your own. For example, if the box holder's name is John Smith, you change the first name to George Smith, or even just the initial G. Again, please note that tampering with another person's mail or mailbox is a federal offense. You should never do this without the person's permission.

There are several advantages to having a private box number with a private agency. You will have a street address, which is sometimes necessary and certainly handy to have. Also, private providers are often open longer hours than the federal government's post office.

Of course, there are disadvantages as well. There are lesser forms than required by the government, but you still have to provide private information and sign a statement that you are supplying correct information. You also commonly need to furnish two forms of identification. However, this type of information is normally well protected by the government, though there are exceptions.

chapter 10

Private Investigators and the Police

Now that you know how you should keep your new identity hidden, it will also help you to understand the processes and tools employed by professionals who might be looking for you. This will help you stay out of their searches and warn you when you may be close to being found.

It is not the average family member or close friend who is going to try to find you. Your threat from those people is severely limited, as they do not know how to go about finding people. They almost certainly do not have the time or resources to devote to a full-time search for a missing person.

Though resources may not stop parents or spouses from looking for you or contacting others who may be able to help, the real threat to your anonymity comes from the professionals — people who are employed to do this kind of work and have experience doing it successfully. The best defense is to know some of the methods professionals use to locate missing persons. If the police are looking for you, you most likely have far less to fear than if private investigators are doing the searching. Police have limited resources, and admit that voluntarily missing people are generally not a priority.

You have to put yourself in the mindset of a professional and figure out how they work. Private investigators, or "skip tracers," make their living trying to find you. This gives them plenty of motivation, and they are not burdened by any emotional attachment to you like a loved one is. They have a clear head and will be able to focus much better than an angry or sad family member.

How Private Investigators Will Search for You

Many private investigators are hired by credit agencies to find people who are in debt and have disappeared. Therefore, many of their techniques are related to financial information, such as your credit report, bank accounts, and bills. This is why it is extremely important to stay out of debt as a voluntary missing person, as well as why running away from a large amount of debt is pointless. Any delinquencies are sent to debt collectors, which creates a track record and a motivated enemy. If your debt is especially high, you will be found.

As a voluntary missing person, you have a great advantage. Private investigators rely on the missing person to still have contact with family and friends, and often call them or write to them under a false pretense to gain your information. If you do not contact your friends or family, you have dried up a large resource. However, just because they do not know your new information does not mean your old information is still not useful. Your loved ones know your personality, which means they may figure out your preferences for new locations to live, jobs you might hold, and even names you could chose. It is very important to completely change habits and tastes as much as possible to avoid any predictable patterns.

A professional investigator is often far more successful than police because he or she will engage family members in the search. Often, the investigator encourages relatives and friends to participate in every avenue of the search. Also, he or she has the ability to aggressively pursue media exposure in local television and print and even, at times, national media, such as CNN, NBC, and 48 Hours.

The typical investigator on the scene will start by interviewing family members and friends to look for clues or even possible reasons why someone has left. There are many available clues from these interviews. If an investigator knows, for example, that someone left because of financial problems, he can narrow the search to financial records left behind. Private investigators can also determine likely destinations for the missing person by asking friends and family members interview questions, such as what areas of the world he or she talked about visiting.

Some investigators still do things the old-fashioned way by locating your last-known street address, for example, and obtaining a list of everyone who lives in the area. Then, he or she can knock on doors and ask questions. If you have done your homework and not told anybody of your plans, this should not present a problem.

Many investigators looking for you start off by doing it in the comfort of their home or office by looking at the various free resources available on the Web, such as on Black Book Online (**www.blackbookonline.info**), which is a search tool that provides access to public and criminal records. The more information they can gather, the better their chances of finding you. First and last names are the best clues. Additional or middle names are also useful. The cities and states where you live or lived last are also valuable clues. The likelihood is that you were not careless enough to join growing profile movements, such as MySpace, but perhaps a teenage son or daughter joined these groups.

Most missing people end up in the United States, but there are cases in which investigators believe the missing person may be living somewhere else in the world. Obviously, these cases involve much more money and time; therefore, the success rate is much lower. The odds of remaining undiscovered are better if you decide to leave the United States than if you stay. Unless investigators have specific information, it is going to be very difficult for them to be successful.

There are all kinds of public records that investigators will comb through in their efforts to find you. If those looking for you know the common area of your new home, here are some records they will find useful, and therefore, areas where you want to avoid having your name appear:

- **Grantor and grantee indexes and records**: These are particularly useful if a private investigator or other searcher knows you own a home. "Grantor" and "grantee" refer to the two main parties involved in the transfer of a title or deed of trust, normally for a home or parcel of land. These are often county records when homes are bought and sold.

- **Reconveyance records:** These records are created when someone takes out a second mortgage on their home. Investigators armed with information can locate who holds the mortgage. These mortgages often have document identification numbers that can be used to trace the borrower. The lesson here is obvious: *Do not take out a second mortgage.*

- **Court dockets:** Court proceedings often found at the county and state level contain information about missing persons. This data comes in raw form, but someone skilled at interpreting it might find it helpful.

- **Uniform commercial code records:** If you own a business, your name will likely appear on their lists. Investigators also can find other information about you, including your address, which is another good reason for using a post office box and not a physical address.

- **Better Business Bureau records:** Even if you own a nonmember business, you might turn up here if someone files a complaint or has some other record of your business.

Outside of a traditional law enforcement approach, private investigators can pursue many alternative avenues. Some private investigators work exclusively on missing adults. They can work exclusively on a handful of cases. Their track records vary, of course, but are almost invariably more successful than county, city, and state police agencies and the FBI. The police have enormous caseloads, so manpower and resources are spread thin, as opposed to a private investigator who may be looking at a handful of cases with plenty of time to spend looking for you.

Investigators have their own individual methods, but the type of information they are seeking frequently includes these elements:

- Full birth name
- Date of birth
- Social security number
- High school
- Year graduated
- Date discharged from U.S. military (if applicable)
- Rank at discharge (if applicable)
- Last known good address
- Year address was valid
- Last employer
- Last profession
- Acquaintances
- Marital status
- Married name
- Spouse or ex-spouse's name

Some private investigators like to use voter registration searches to help find a missing person. Voter files contain names and addresses and also, at times, the social security number. Much of this computerized information is new, which is to the advantage of the investigator. Of course, if you have not registered to vote, this should not be problem.

Another popular technique is to look up a driver's license and view the records. Some online information services offer this information for a fee, depending which state the investigator is looking in. If you happen to be pulled over and receive any kind of mark on your license, that information is often easily obtainable with only your driver's license number, and the private investigator can see the date and location of your infraction. If the investigator does not have your correct name, it will be nearly impossible to find you.

Limit the resources for private investigators

It is not realistic to think you can delete or deter private investigators and others looking for information about you at all these sites. You cannot eliminate every risk, but you can turn the odds in your favor. There are a variety of ways they can find you, such as through your phone system. It is a good idea to use one phone for incoming calls and another for outgoing communications, change the numbers regularly, and dump the old telephones. Also, route your utility and other bills through a corporation to help deter someone who wants to use those records to find you.

The more information an investigator can gather about you, the better his or her chances of finding you. You want to avoid leaving behind what are sometimes called "identifiers," or your personal information. Investigators separate you from others with the same name through your particular personal information, using what is essentially an elimination process.

A common mistake is for people to often leave a paper trail that can be useful in tracking, such as driver's license information or a license plate number. People also often forget and leave behind bills or credit information.

Your profession can also tip off an investigator. Someone who was a nurse or hairdresser in a previous life might return to that profession. Investigators who perhaps identify where a missing nurse lives might begin their searches at local hospitals, for example. It is always a good idea to change your profession, if at all possible; however, this is not always feasible.

Investigators say the way most people get caught is simple — they cannot leave their old life behind. You are advised not to take up your previous occupation, hobbies, or habits. If you are a well-known matchbook collector, for example, find a new hobby. If you are known for frequenting coffee houses, start going to church socials or wine-connoisseur socials. Another easy way for investigators to find you is if you talk about or mention your past to strangers, or even friends. Do not talk about your past.

Investigators have gotten much more sophisticated in their methods these days. Similar to used car dealers, some investigators even offer "Guaranteed Locate Plans." Essentially, this means they either find the missing person, or there is no charge. There are frequently strings attached to the plan, though, and its success rate is not known. Some agencies also offer flat-fee rates with guaranteed prices, but these may lead to the suggestion that more advanced services be purchased.

Dealing with Police Officers

Before you hide, you should determine your biggest threat of being found. Consider who will look for you and how serious their efforts may be. Do not underestimate them. It is possible that no professionals will be looking for you, but to feel safer, you should be aware of the threat of exposure, not just from private investigators, but from the police. If they are not sure your disappearance was voluntary, their efforts to find you will be more pressed. The police have limited resources, so they will obviously want to search for someone who may have been kidnapped or harmed rather than someone who chose to leave his or her life behind. Private investigators stop looking for you once they are not being paid anymore, but the police could always find you, even if they are not intentionally looking.

Police officers make judgments about character when it comes to who they stop and why. Obviously if you are driving erratically, there is a reason to stop you because you are endangering yourself and others. You do not want to arouse any suspicion. Do not display any signs of nervousness, exceed the speed limit, or do anything else that might create curiosity if you happen to be in sight of a conscientious cop.

Another obvious way of raising possible suspicions is to have all your possessions in your car. If you happen to get stopped by a police officer, or if one merely drives by you, you do not want to look like you have packed up your possessions. Even if you are just a passing memory, the officer who noticed your possession-filled car might remember it later if word gets out that you have vanished. Always try to blend in.

If you are ever pulled over by a cop, act normal. Pull over and stop in a safe area, and turn the engine off. Wait calmly with your hands in view, usually on the steering wheel is considered standard. Do nothing unless prompted by the officer. Even though you know he or she is going to ask for your license and registration, wait until asked to retrieve it. Remember, this officer has no idea who you are and might think you are reaching for a weapon. Never speak first, and answer politely and succinctly. Do not try to explain your way out of the ticket or demand anything from the officer. Even if you believe the officer is in the wrong, you will not want to pursue any legal action as someone who is attempting to stay hidden.

There are certain times when an officer can legally search your car without consent. If an officer can see illegal items, such as drugs or an open alcohol container, he or she can search your car. If you move in a way that suggests you are hiding something, such as reaching under your seat, the officer can search your car. As a voluntary missing person, this is last thing you want, but there is little you can do besides avoid being pulled over to begin with.

If you run, you could get hurt, and you will be arrested. Most of the time, these stops are routine. Remind yourself that it is unlikely the police officer has any unusual reason to stop you. The officer might be stopping you for a broken taillight, for example.

Maintain your car to minimize the possibility of being stopped for an automobile violation. Make sure all the lights work. Your biggest problem in the end may be traffic stops and check points. They can happen anytime, without any notice. There is not much you can do except try to avoid them.

You could also listen to the radio and traffic reports. News reports often inform viewers or listeners of police activity or may even inform you of a roadblock. There are also radars you can have in your car that detect police scanners, but be sure they are legal in your state.

Also, try to avoid traveling during holidays. Police are out in full force during those times. Although it is considered unconstitutional to pull vehicles over and conduct searches without probable cause, officers still do this sometimes. Studies show this happens most often during holidays.

Using public transportation or a taxi might be a safer bet. Police usually do not stop these, and they routinely pass through police checkpoints with ease. So it is a good idea to use public transit whenever you can.

Increasingly, local police are using social networking sites, like Facebook and MySpace, to help track down missing people. Although these sites mainly are used to look for missing young people who may not have disappeared voluntarily, it is something you should be aware of.

Police authorities are generally getting more computer-savvy, and the Internet, as you read earlier, is increasingly being used as a means to track down those who do not want to be found.

Police-friendly sites, such as the National Center for Missing Adults (**www.theyaremissed.org/ncma**), are also reliable resources. This site advertises that it is free and offers a vast variety of information on missing people.

In 2004, Britain started a program of putting the faces of the most dangerous criminals on the Internet as part of a "crime stopper" program. This is similar to the FBI-style "Most Wanted" Web site. This was the first time British police were able to post details of its most wanted criminals online. Even though these target wanted criminals, it would not be surprising if the next step was to post all missing people, or at least those individuals whose photos are available to the police.

Police searches

One common misconception about filing a missing persons report is that there is a waiting period if the person is an adult. This is no longer true — someone can file a missing persons report as soon as he or she suspects you are gone. No two police forces in the United States have the same list of initial actions they take when someone is reported missing, but these are common:

- Question the informant about the nature of the disappearance.
- Discuss the missing person's possible reasons for leaving.
- Obtain information on the person's hobbies, occupation, and personal habits.
- Obtain a recent photograph.
- Get a list of associates, friends, and relatives.
- Conduct a thorough search of the missing person's normal place of residence and other locations.
- Assess the possibility of foul play and bring it to the attention of supervisor.

- Make an initial assessment of the potential harm that may come to the missing person.
- Check whether the missing person is in police custody.
- Check local hospitals.
- Fill out a missing person form, giving details of the missing person and actions taken.
- Check relevant police indexes and intelligence systems for evidence of the person being "at risk" of abuse or violence.
- Check of relevant non-police indexes, such as the local social services' "at risk" register.
- Check of force crimes recording systems for information that the missing person may be an offender, a vulnerable witness, or a crime victim.
- Check the missing person index for previous incidents of the same nature.
- Circulate the description of the missing person to police patrols.

Police emphasize crime, not people who voluntarily disappear. If you are careful about covering all traces to your future home, you are almost sure to avoid the casual detective work of the local police force.

As for your chances of being found by someone other than the police, the key issue here is how hard someone is going to try to find you. It is partly a function of time and money. If those who want to find you have access to both, be extra careful.

In many cases, police and private investigators are not the primary concern. It is financial institutions. These are super-bureaus, such as Equifax, that collect information from credit card companies, banks, insurance carriers, and the government itself. When vanished people are found, it is often through their efforts. Just about any financial transaction you make is fed back into credit bureau files, which are updated daily. This data is sometimes sold to private companies at a cost of pennies per record.

Your financial data can appear in a variety of places, so before you disappear, make sure you have left no financial information behind. Common sources include:

- Credit unions
- Individual Retirement Accounts (IRAs)
- Employers
- Stockbrokers and agencies
- Banks and Savings associations
- 401(k) Plans
- Separate Employment Plans (SEPs)
- Insurance policies
- Annuities and investments
- Business entities
- Credit cards

The Prospect of Amateurs Finding You

This chapter primarily discusses the various ways professionals could locate you, but you should also consider what "amateurs" or relatives might attempt to do on their own. Their investigations will almost certainly be limited because of time and money constraints, but you should still be aware of this possibility.

How easy it is for someone to find you depends on what he or she knows about you and how effectively he or she uses that knowledge. For example, if they know your social security number, they might be able to track you in a few minutes. This is not likely, though, particularly because you have been careful to cover your tracks. If searchers know your name and date of birth, they can find you in a few hours. If you followed the steps in this book, you have another name, so this should not be a problem.

Some desperate amateurs turn to Web sites, which advertise that for around $40 or so, they can "find anyone." They are virtually useless, if not outright scams. Many simply provide lists of old addresses. These usually never lead to positive results.

The bottom line is that relatives and friends may make half-hearted searches for you, but it is highly unlikely they will succeed, assuming you took all precautions outlined in this book.

Various Web sites about missing persons might uncover your whereabouts. Many of these are geared toward non-voluntary absences, such as kidnappings, but they have the potential of turning up someone who chooses to be missing as well. One of these is SomeoneIsMissing.com (**http://someoneismissing.com**), which promises to supply the following resources to families or others who are searching for missing persons:

- A Web address
- Web space
- The site's resources for as long as necessary

- Resources to handle press and media
- Information on the site provided by you about the missing person
- Internet exposure

The site says it is free and describes its mission as providing, "instant Internet exposure for missing persons of any age, race, or religion worldwide."

If you have read this far in the book, you know the Internet is both a great tool and a powerful enemy. Your name will almost certainly show up if someone has a clue where to look. As you will see, though, there are ways to obscure or minimize, if not erase, your name from Internet files.

Candid private investigators will tell you it is not Google or Yahoo! that you should fear the most. Rather, it is sites, such as ZabaSearch (**www.zabasearch.com**). This is a controversial site, but it works. The site searches for, and lists, different types of information of U.S. citizens, including current and past addresses, phone numbers, and birth years.

Try this yourself. Input your name on ZabaSearch and see what happens. No matter how obscure you think you are, you may have several pages of listings. A headline at the top of the page says this is a "detailed background report" with information, such as criminal records and contact information. Each listing will have your name, often with a different address.

Perhaps in part because of public opinion concerns, ZabaSearch offers a free service that e-mails an alert any time your name is submitted in a search. The alert will also provide a geographical location of the person looking you up. "Your e-mail address will not be used for any other purpose and will be deleted," ZabaSearch says. In the case of ZabaSearch, you have a way of monitoring a potential threat, which is not always the case with Internet searching.

One of the easiest and most commonly accessed sites is the newspaper, which often has records of births, deaths, and in some cases, neighborhood news that may be about a place where you have lived. If you know you have appeared in, say, the local weekly newspaper, try contacting a friend to see if your name can be removed before you leave. If that is not possible, there is not much you can do about it, but it is something you should be aware of.

In recent years there are a variety of sites, which have been developed with the main purpose of finding people. One example is Net Detective (**www.netdetective.com**), which promises to find people and searches a database of more than 211 million U.S. residents. The site is one of many that do anything from searching for your whereabouts to locating unlisted telephone numbers. However, if you follow the suggestions in this book, you will have a better chance of not being found.

chapter 11

Reclaiming Your Old Identity

What if you realize that running away from your old life was a huge mistake? Or, what if you are found and forced back into it? Every situation varies, but if you willingly return, it is possible friends and relatives could harbor a grudge regarding your decision to disappear. Even if they knew you were alive and safe, they could feel that you made the choice that they were less important than the issue that caused you to flee. If you left because of abuse, you can contact other friends or loved ones temporarily once you have left town, but you choose your contact carefully. The safest bet is to use intermediaries. Even if you know this person would never intentionally betray your information, they could still accidentally release it.

If you decide to meet your loved one in person, a neutral place far from your present location is the best choice. Consider an amusement park or mall where you can see from a distance whether they brought friends. Remember, there is a correlation between your chances of staying invisible and the number of people who might be able to trace you or who already know where you are.

Almost invariably, you have given some thought to those left behind. You might consider doing this more for them than for yourself. Your loved ones are going to wonder about you — whether you are alive or dead, whether you are healthy and doing well, or whether you are depressed. Remember, families of missing people have continuing needs for advice, practical help, and emotional support. Many choose to get professional counseling.

Practical matters on your return include some touchy legal issues. For example, say your heirs were receiving social security as a result of your presumed demise. Your return will mean the government will want some answers and may demand repayment. There have been bitter battles in cases in which trials had to be completed to settle who was allocated the assets of a vanished individual who came back.

If you do decide to reunite with your family, do not expect them to embrace you with open arms. They have not even been allowed to attend a funeral service to say goodbye to you. There may be some resentment at first. If you have been gone for years, you will face even more serious issues with friends and family than if you returned within weeks or months. Be prepared to answer a slew of questions.

The most obvious question you should prepare for is, "Why did you leave?" The next question is usually along the lines of, "Will you do it again?" You have to understand that some family members will be preoccupied with these questions, and it can be very difficult to make sense of the situation. You will have to effectively communicate the desperate state that caused you to leave.

Remember that while you disappeared, your relationship did not. You may face a situation in which your left-behind family finally got over their anxiety and concerns about you and began to heal. Your return may bring some ambivalent feelings. What if they had written you off as gone, perhaps dead, and now you are back? Feelings of disbelief when you return is a natural part of the process.

Things Moved on Without You

If you have returned, remember that you have changed, but so have your loved ones. They may even have different personalities. You will also have to face the possibility that while you were absent, family members may have embraced new hobbies, habits, and attitudes. This can be difficult to accept and understand.

Another factor to consider is that not all families will welcome you back. You might have to earn their trust and acceptance because they have written you off as being dead or out of the family picture. Some families may not wish to be reunited with you or have any more contact because of the pain you caused.

Health practitioners say the experience of loved ones while you were away is a critical component in your acceptance back into the fold. Studies show that families who managed to function well, carved out happy lives, and had a positive outlook after you left, find it easiest to transition when you return. It will be much harder for you to successfully reunite with family members if they have not been able to reach what some experts describe as an "emotional maturity."

There is not an easy way to cope with your return or make your relationships what they once were. You may need to see mental health specialists to facilitate the process. The guidance of an experienced practitioner can help ease any necessary adjustments.

You also need to realize that however long you have been away, it makes no sense to return to your old life if you are still uncomfortable with "the way it was." Perhaps your situation during your absence has changed, or perhaps you have changed, and you can make an intelligent decision about whether you want to return.

Regaining Their Trust

There are some things you can do to slowly regain the trust of your loved ones. First, you should all talk about your decision to leave openly, possibly with a professional counselor. If the subject is treated as taboo and never discussed, there will always be lingering questions and suppressed feelings. Once they understand why you decided to leave and come back, even if they do not agree with your choices, they can begin to forgive you.

A few basic methods for regaining the trust of loved ones include:

- Be consistent and reliable. You must demonstrate that you will always stick by your word and keep your promises before people trust you will behave the way you say you will. This way, when you say "I will not run away again," people will believe you.

- It may seem obvious, but do not keep secrets. You will need to learn how to be open and honest with your loved ones because you will be under scrutiny for a long time, possibly the rest of your life. This does not mean your life has to be completely transparent, but do not lie about things like where you are going and who you are with. They should respect your privacy when it comes to things like dating, but tell them you are on a date — not that you are working late.

- Obey the golden rule — treat people the way you want to be treated. If you worry that your family does not trust you and you act accordingly, they will not trust you. Be confident and they will reflect that confidence back at you. Do not get defensive and demand to be trusted when wrongfully accused. Although you may grow weary of not initially being trusted, be patient and stick with it because they will have no choice but to come around.

How to Cope if You Are Not Welcome

What if your loved ones refuse to let you back into their lives? You will have to cope with the loss and move on. You knew it was a risk when you left, but the reality may be harder than you expected. You have to try to move on and build a new life. In a way, it is similar to losing a loved one. You do not stop loving them or cherishing their memory, but you have to continue on with your life. You should not cling to the idea that your family and friends will change their minds, but they may, so if you are happy and well adjustedm you will be able to rejoin them much more easily than if you are upset about initially being rejected.

First, accept the reality of the situation. Do not obsess about being forgiven, even if it is a possibility down the road. Believe it or not, even your own mother refuses to talk to you, you can move on and the feelings of grief will pass. Otherwise, no one would be able to survive the death of a loved one. This may seem strange or immoral, but if the situation is truly out of your hands, you should not punish yourself for the rest of your life. If you read the beginning of this book before leaving, then you truly considered your reasons for leaving and believed disappearance was the best option. Any time you are sad or miss the person, acknowledge your feelings and move on. Do not punish yourself by thinking you caused yourself this pain, so you must keep hurting. This person chose to stop speaking to you, not the other way around.

If you need to speak to someone from your past, write a letter you will not send. This provides a physical outlet that allows you to release some of your emotions. Even better, you can talk to a counselor and tell him or her what you wish to say to the person in question. Being able to express the words out loud is often enough to help comfort yourself.

You should also participate in healthy activities that draw focus away from your grief or anger. Getting a hobby, especially a physically demanding one, will help you feel alive and connected to the world. Exercise keeps you healthy and gets endorphins pumping through your system that actually affect your emotions in a positive way. Unhealthy activities, such a drug use may seem to make everything better, but they a bandage that only covers the problem and does not treat the issue. Healthy hobbies act like stitches, closing your wounds so they can heal properly.

conclusion

We hope the information in this book helps you greatly improve your life. The process of becoming a voluntary missing person is long and sometimes complicated. If deem it necessary to remain happy and free, then this book has provided you a plan to disappear. The process of becoming a missing person forces you to change your life and consider what you absolutely cannot be without. We wish you luck in finding the freedom or happiness that was unattainable in your old life.

appendix a

Tax Haven Resources

There are a number of great organizations worldwide that can help you find further information regarding tax haven regulations in their countries.

Offshore Tax Consultants

United Kingdom

Tax Consultants Fund
Info Guide Publications, Ltd.
Mayfair House
14-18 Heddon St.
Mayfair
London
W1B 4DA
Phone: +44 (0871) 504-5532
E-mail: info@taxconsultants-guide.com

Clark & Co.
12 North Hill
Colchester
Essex
CO1 1AS
Phone: +44 (0120) 657-7422
Fax: +44 (0120) 656-2816
E-mail: partners@clarke-colchester.co.uk

Citycas Ltd.
Valiant House

4-10 Heneage Lane
London
CO1 1AS
Phone: +44 (0207) 626-7171
Fax: +44 (0207) 626-7272
E-mail: info@citycas.com

MD Consulting Limited
St Mary's Court
The Broadway
Amersham
Buckinghamshire
HP7 0UT
Phone: +44 (0149) 477-2765

Taxation Web Ltd.
6 Coleby Avenue
Peel Hall
Manchester
M22 5HH
United Kingdom
Mark McLaughlin
E-mail: martino@taxationweb.co.uk

The Wells Partnership
The Old Rectory, Church Street
Weybridge
Surrey
KT13 8DE
England
Phone: +44 (0193) 270-4700
Fax: +44 (0193) 285-5049

Berg Kaprow Lewis
35 Ballards Lane
London
Greater London
N3 1XW
England
Phone: +44 (0208) 922-9222
Fax: +44 (0208) 922-9223

Greenwood Barton
National Westminster Bank Chambers
Heckmondwike
West Yorkshire
WF16 0HU
England

Bartlett Kershaw Trott
4 Pullman Court, Great Western Road
Gloucester
Gloucestershire
GL1 3ND
England
Phone: +44 (0145) 252-7000
Fax: +44 (0145) 230-4585

Harris Lipman
2 Mountainview Court, 310 Friern Barnet Lane
Whetstone
London
N20 0YZ

England
Phone: +44 (0208) 446-9000
Fax: +44 (0208) 446-9537

Maskell, Moss, & Co. Limited
24 Cathedral Road
Cardiff
South lamorgan
CF11 9LJ
Wales
Phone: +44 (0292) 025-6330
Fax: +44 (0292) 025-6331

The Institute of Chartered Accountants in Ireland
CA House, 87/89 Pembroke Rd.
Dublin
Ir 4
Ireland
Phone: +353 1-637-7200
Fax: +353 1-668-0842

Conway, Conway & Co.
12 Basin St
Nass
Co. Kildare
KD
Ireland

Isle of Man

Isle of Man – Head Office
OCRA (Isle of Man) Limited
Grosvenor Court
Tower Street
Ramsey, Isle of Man IM8 1JA
British Isles
Phone: +44(1624) 811000
Fax: +44(1624) 811001
E-mail: Stevenson@ocra.com
Contacts: David Stevenson, Colin Forster, Brian Monk

Italy

Faulkner International Ltd.
Italy, Rome
Vio Carlo Passaglia No 11
Rome
Italy
Senior Financial Consultant
E-mail: johnmpye@faulkner-international.com

Faulkner International Ltd.
Italy Turin
Piemont
Turin
Italy
Financial Consultant E-mail: david.silk@faulkner-international.com

Mary Jan Bridges
Via Urbana 116, 00184 Rome

Phone: +39 06-474-7069

Donald J. Carroll
Largo Angelo Fochetti 28, 00154 Rome
Phone: +39 06-570-281
Fax: +39 06-570-2827-33
E-mail: donald.carroll@studiopirola.com

Cynthia J. Ehrlich
Via Cassia 595/F, 00189 Rome
Phone: +39 06-336-0340
E-mail: USTAXhelp@yahoo.com

Timothy Ellis
Via Paolo V 11 - Int. 7, 00167 Rome
Phone: +39 06-614-3216

Vincent P. Gambino
Via Asiago 1, 00195 Rome
Phone: +39 06-3751-1192
Fax: +39 06-3741-1420
E-mail: VPGambino@tiscalinet.it.

Sally M. Silvers
Via Basento 37, 00198 Rome
Phone: +39 06-853-57172
E-mail: sally.silvers@flashnet.it

France

Faulkner International Ltd.
France, Paris
Faulkner Counseil SARL
116, Avenue du General Leclerc
75014 Paris
France
E-mail: info@faulkner-international.com

Faulkner International Ltd.
France, Valbone
Faulkner Conseil SARL
6, Rue Soutrane, 1er Etage
06560 Valbonne
France
Regional Director E-mail: terry.hurley@faulkner-international.com

Czech Republic

Faulkner International Ltd.
Czech Republic
p.a. On-Target
Perlova 1 110 00 Prague 1
Czech Republic
Financial Consultant E-mail: david.newton@faulkner-international.com

Tax Consultants Guide

Info Guide Publications
Lindenstrasse 2
Glenhausen
Frankfurt
Germany
63571
Phone: +49 6051-618140
E-mail: info@taxconsultants-guide.com

Norway

Faulkner International Ltd.
Norway
Proffice, Lokkeveien 10,
400 Stavaner,
Norway
E-mail: ian.neil@faulkner-international.com, steve.calloway@faulkner-international.com

Brazil

Faulkner International Ltd.
Brazil
Traversa do Ouvidor 50 (sobreloja)
Centro 20040 – 040 Rio De Janeiro
Brazil
Regional Director E-mail: tim.richards@faulkner-international.com
http://faulkner-international.com

Faulkner International Ltd
Brazil
Rua Haddock Lobo 846
Conjunctura 1105
Edificio Netware
Cerqueira Cesar
01414-000 Sao Paulo
Brazil
Regional Director E-mail: robin.saunders@faulkner-international.com
Consultant E-mail: info@faulkner-international.com

Netherlands

Faulkner International Ltd.
Netherlands, Eindhoven
Faulkner Nederland BV
Fellenoord 130, 5611ZB
Eindhoven
Netherlands
E-mail: info@faulkner-international.com

Faulkner International Lrd
Netherlands, Hoofddorp

Faulkner Nederland BV
De Horsten, Planetenweg 15A
2132HN Hoofddorp
Netherlands
Financial Consultant E-mail: clive.anderton@faulkner-international.com

Vietnam

Faulkner International Ltd.
Vietnam
Ho Chi Minh
Vietnam
Financial Consultant E-mail: keith.bridger@faulkner-international.com

Bahain

Faulkner International Ltd.
Kingdom of Bahrain
Manama
Kingdom of Bahrain
Regional Director E-mail: chris.watts@faulkner-international.com

Latvia

Faulkner International Ltd.
Latvia
Latvia
E-mail: into@faulkner-international.com

Russia

Faulkner International Ltd.
Moscow
Moscow
E-mail: info@faulkner-international.com

Dubai

Faulkner International Ltd
Dubai
Apt 307, Obedulla Tower
PO Box 52465
Bur Dubai
Dubai
United Arab Emirates
Regional Director E-mail: eric.boardman@faulkner-international.com

Thailand

Faulkner International Ltd.
Thailand
Bamboo Court Apartment 5
59-38 Sukumvit Soi 26
Klongtoey
Bangkok 10110
Thailand

Regional Director E-mail: john.
macgill@faulkner-interna-
tional.com

China

Faulkner International Ltd.
China, Shenzhen
1 Gong Ye 1st Rd
Shekou Industrial Zone
518069 Shenzhen
The People's Repulic of China
E-mail: info@faulkner-interna-
tional.com

Faulkner International Ltd.
China, Shanghai
14C No:1051, Xin Zha Road
Jing An District
Shanghai 200041
The People's Republic of
China
Regional Director E-mail:
brian.mcandrew@faulkner-
international.com

OCRA (Hong Kong) Limited
3908 Two Exchange Square
8 Connaught Place
Central
Hong Kong
Phone: +852 2522-0172
Fax: +852 2522-4720
E-mail: hongkong@ocra.com.
hk
Bart Dekker
Iris Les

South Korea

Faulkner International Ltd.
Korea
Seoul
Korea
E-mail: info@faulkner-interna-
tional.com

Japan

Faulkner International Ltd.
Japan
9F Motoakasaka Building
1-7-10 Motoakasaka
Minato-Ku
Tokyo, 107-0051
Japan
Financial Consultants E-mail:
asher.lepcha@faulkner-interna-
tional.com

Switzerland

Faulkner International Ltd.
Switzerland, Geneva
MPM Geneva (European Inter-
national Office)

Avenue Louis-Casai 18
1211 Geneva 28
Switzerland
E-mail: info@faulkner-international.com

Faulkner International Ltd.
Switzerland, Basle
Basle
Switzerland
E-mail: info@faulkner-international.com

Spain

Faulkner international Ltd.
Spain
World Trade Center
Edifico Sur - 2a Planta
Muelle de Barcelona
Barcelona, 08039
Spain
Regional Director E-mail: paul.evans@faulkner-international.com
Training Manager E-mail: steve.carter@faulkner-international.com

Australia

Ten-Forty Tax Preparation
P.O. Box 988
Bondi Junction, NSW 1355
Richard Grilliot
E-mail: tenforty@bigpond.net.au

Expatriate Tax Associates
1 Grove Street
Birchgrove, NSW 2041
E-mail: evanhill@extax.com.au
www.extax.com.au
Phone: +61 9555-5663
Fax: +61 9810-0557

Ernst & Young
321 Kent Street
Sydney, NSW 2001
G.S. Choong or Ron Crowe
Phone: +61 9248-5555
Fax: +61 9248-5314

Taylor Woodings Corporate Services
Level 26 Royal Exchange Building, 56 Pitt Street
Sydney
New South Wales, Australia
1225
International
Phone: +61 (02) 8247-8000
Fax: +61 (02) 8247-8099

Price Waterhouse Coopers
201 Kent St.

Sydney, NSW 2000
GPO Box 4177
Sydney NSW 2001
Jim Tait: +61 8266-2992
Helen Cudlipp: +61 8266-2995
Carol Separovich: +61 8266-5769
Rohan Geddes: +61 8266-7261
Fax: +61 8266-8910

Walter Jacenko
P.O. Box 247
Eastwood, NSW 2122
Phone: +61 9874-4558
Fax: +61 9874-6440

U.S. Tax Management P/L
1907/1 Sergeants Lane
St. Leonards NSW 2065
Al Simpson
E-mail: alsimpson@bigpond.com
Phone: +61 9906-2633
Fax: +61 9906-2644

KPMG
KPMG Centre
45 Clarence St.
Sydney, NSW 2000
GPO Box H67 Australia Square
Sydney, NSW 2000
Rodney Moor
Phone: +61 9335-8202
Fax: +61 9299-7077

Darrel Casubrook
Causbrook & Associates
Suite 1204, Level 12
66 King Street
Sydney NSW 2000
E-mail: darrel.causbrook@causbrooks.com.au
Phone: +61 9299-1850
Fax: +61 9299-1860

Richard A. Bobb
155 Castlereagh Street
7th Floor
Sydney, NSW 2000
Richard Bobb or Kathryn Chow
Phone: +61 9261-2422
Fax: +61 9264-8701

Deloitte Ross Tohmatsu
255 George Street
Sydney, NSW 2000
C.J. Getz
Phone: +61 9322-7680
Fax: +61 9322-7025

Harry V. Turner & Co.
Suite 25
105 Longueville Rd.
Lane Cove, NSW 2066
P.O. Box 673

Lane Cove, NSW 1595
Harry Turner
Phone: +61 9427-0599 or +61 9427-0818
Fax: +61 9427–5976

Teresea D. West
C/- Cropper Parkhill Solicitors
Level 20, 1 Castlereagh Street
Sydney, NSW 2000
(P.O. Box 71 Burwood, NSW 2134)
Mobile: +61 0418-681-284
Phone: +61 9232-5000

Duthre Samurai & Co. Pty Ltd.
Charles A Duthie
P.O. Box 97
Lane Cove, NSW 2066
Phone: +61 9418-6942
Fax: +61 9418-6855

John L. Campbell
c/o Zein el Hassan
Corrs Chambers Westgarth
Governor Philip Tower
Sydney NSW 2000
John L. Campbell
Phone: +61 9210-6500
Fax: +61 9210-6611
(for estate and gift taxes only)

Australian Capital Territory
Duesburys Chartered Accountants
7th Floor St. George Bank Building
60 Marcus Clarke Street
Canberra, ACT 2601
GPO Box 500
Canberra, ACT 2601
Phone: +61 (02) 6279-5400
Fax: +61 (02) 6279-5444
Michelle Horner: U.S. Tax Specialist

Hallett and Company
Level 8 AMP Tower
1 Hobart Place
Canberra City, ACT 2602
Phone: +61 (02) 6257-5712
Fax: +61 (02) 6257-5958
Peter Radford: U.S. Tax Specialist

Queensland KPMG
345 Queen Street, Level 30
Brisband, Qld 4000
GPO Box 223
Brisbane, Qld 4001
Bill Armagnacq
Phone: +61 (07) 3233-3111
Fax: +61 (07) 322-0074

Perth

The Tax Lady
5 Malcom Court
Noranda, WA 6062
Phone: +61 (08) 9375-5946
E-mail: marv@starwon.com.au

U.S. National Tax Associations

The following contacts can be used to find out more information on how your taxes will be affected by a move to another country or how to legally move to another country while still settling your taxes.

U.S. Accounting Associations:
www.taxsites.com/associations2.html#accounting-us

American Bar Association – Section of Taxation:
www.abanet.org/tax/home.html

American College of Trust and Estate Counsel:
www.actec.org

American Institute of Certified Public Accountants:
www.aicpa.org

American Payroll Association:
www.americanpayroll.org

American Property Tax Counsel:
www.aptcnet.com

American Society of IRS Problem Solvers:
www.irsproblemsolvers.com

American Taxation Association:
http://aaahq.org/ATA/

Appraisers Association of America:
www.appraisersassoc.org/

Association for Computers and Taxation:
http://taxact.org

Center for State and Local Taxation:
www.iga.ucdavis.edu/Research/CSLT

Council on State Taxation:
www.statetax.org

Federation of Tax Administrators:
www.taxadmin.org

Institute for Professionals in Taxation:
www.ipt.org

Multistate Tax Commission:
www.mtc.gov

National Association of Computerized Tax Processors:
www.nactp.org

National Association of Enrolled Agents:
www.naea.org

National Association of State Auditors, Comptrollers and Treasurers: **www.nasact.org**

National Association of State Budget Officers:
www.nasbo.org

National Association of Tax Consultants:
www.natctax.org

National Association of Tax Professionals:
www.natptax.com

National Council of Property Taxation:
www.ncpt.net

National Society of Tax Professionals:
www.nstp.org

National Tax Association:
http://ntanet.org

National Taxpayers Conference:
www.statetaxes.net

Tax Executives Institute:
www.tei.org

U.S. State Tax Associations

Alabama Society of EAs

Roland Fricke, EA
P.O. Box 242
Arab, AL 35016
Phone: (256) 586-4111
Fax: (256) 586-4138
E-mail: buddy@bara.net
www.alsea.org

Alaska Society of EAs
H. Joi Soucy, EA
P.O. Box 2163
Kodiak, AK 99615
Phone: (907) 486-6225
Fax: (907) 486-4129
E-mail: msbear@worldnet.att.net

Arizona Society of EAs
Larry Martin, EA
7360 E 22nd St #109
Tucson, AZ 85710
Phone: (520) 722-8363
Fax: (520) 722-8398
E-mail: martinea@juno.com
www.aztaxpros.org

Arkansas Society of EAs
Sherry Main, EA
15493 Riches Rd
Fayetteville, AR 72704
Phone: (479) 521-0310
Fax: (479) 521-2269
E-mail: slmain@nwark.com
www.arksea.org

California Society of EAs
Richard J Quarterman, EA
13204 Myford Road Ste 835
Tustin, CA 92782
Phone: (949) 261-2111
Fax: (949) 261-7070
E-mail: r.quarterman@att.net
www.csea.org

Colorado Society of EAs
Victoria Bell, EA
6535 S. Dayton Street
Englewood, CO 80111
Phone: (303) 708-8077
Fax: (303) 708-8079
E-mail: bellsultax@aol.com
www.taxproco.org

CSEA Executive Office:
Catherine Apker, CAE
Executive Vice President
3200 Ramos Circle
Sacramento, CA 95827
Phone: (916) 366-6646
Fax: (916) 366-6674
E-mail: evp@csea.org

Connecticut Society of EAs
Caroline Frano, EA
1111 E Putnam Ave.
Riverside, CT 06878

Phone: (203) 637-3887
E-mail: caroline.frano@snet.net

Florida Society of EAs
Lynn Schmidt, EA
1495 Sixth Street, SE
Winter Haven, FL 33880
Phone: (863) 295-9895
Fax: (863) 298-8299
E-mail: lynn@lyncotax.com
www.fseaonline.org

FSEA Executive Office: Jean Gates EA
P.O. Box 3895
Clearwater, FL 33767
Phone: (727) 442-2806
Fax: (727) 442-2724
E-mail: taxtiger@gte.net

Georgia Society of EAs
Audrey L. Griffin, EA
Griffin Tax Service
100-C N. Houston Lake Blvd
Centerville, GA 31028-1713
Phone: (478) 953-5016
Fax: (478) 953-6092
E-mail: griftax@grifsolu.com
www.4gaea.org

Hawaii Society of EAs
David Ramirez, EA
P.O. Box 61397
Honolulu, HI 96839-1397
Phone: (808) 589-2322
Fax: (808) 589-2422
E-mail: irstaxrelief@msn.com

Illinois Society of EAs
Karen Miller, EA
496 W. Boughton Road
Bolingbrook, IL 60440
Phone: (630) 759-5070
Fax: (630) 759-9101
E-mail: eataxes@aol.com
www.ilsea.org

Illinois Society of EAs
Executive Director: Jacquelie Meyer, EA
1415 Matanuska Trail
McHenry, IL 60050
Phone: (815) 385-6889
Fax: (815) 363-1623
E-mail: Meyer_JD@msn.com
www.ilsea.org

Indiana Society of EAs
Helen (Casey) Juza, EA
202 E Main Street
Danville, IN 46122
Phone: (317) 745-6051
Fax: (317) 745-1735
E-mail: execserv@aol.com
www.indianaenrolledagents.com

Iowa Society of EAs
David J Adkins, EA
4415 Stone Ave.
Sioux City, IA 51106
Phone: (712) 276-9240
E-mail: Jeff@adkinstax.com

Kentucky Society of EAs
John C Frazier, EA
8333 Alexandria Pike
Suite 204
Alexandria, KY 41101
Phone: (859) 694-3000
Fax: (859) 448-2762
E-mail: jctaxpro@aol.com

Louisiana Society of EAs
Dexter Duhon, EA
114 S. State Street
Abbeville, LA 70510
Phone: (318) 893-2702
Fax: (318) 893-2780
E-mail: djd@msis.net

Maryland/DC Society of EAs
Robert Jacobs, EA
550M Ritchie Hwy, #145
Serverna Park, MD 21146
Phone: (410) 544-4680
Fax: (410) 544-1324
E-mail: ataxguru@prodigy.net

Massachusetts Society of EAs
Leon M. Rudman, EA
39 Powell Street
Stoughton, MA 02072
Phone: (781) 344-9031
Fax: (781) 344-9031
E-mail: rudman@comcast.net
www.maseaonline.org

Michigan Society of EAs
Robert Hemenway, EA
602 West Main Street
Owosso, MI 48867
Phone: (989) 723-5977
Fax: (989) 725-8372
E-mail: hbsowosso@michon-line.net

MiSEA Administrative Office
1071 E Nine Mile Rd
Hazel Park, MI 48030
Phone: (248) 547-9934
Fax: (248) 547-9934

Minnesota Society of EAs
Dorothy Anderson, EA
P.O. Box 748
Crosslake, MN 56442
Phone: (218) 692-2650
Fax: (218) 692-3364
E-mail: aceinc@crosslake.net
www.mnsea.org

Mississippi Society of EAs

Bertha Page, EA
615 West Canal Street
Picayune, MS 39466-3916
Phone: (601) 798-3116
Fax: (601) 798-5650
E-mail: pagetax@datasync.com

Missouri Society of EAs
James Bales, EA
1800 Liberty Park Blvd, #6
Sedalia, MO 65301
Phone: (660) 827-3212
E-mail: taxpro@iland.net
www.mosea.org

Nevada Society of EAs
Cherene D. Cooper, EA
2585 S. Jones Blvd, Ste 2D
Las Vegas, NV 89146-5604
Phone: (702) 646-4646
Fax: (702) 364-4697
E-mail: cherene.cooper@gte.net

New Mexico Society of EAs
Linda Ruckel, EA
3900 Paseo del Sol
Santa Fe, NM 87507
Phone: (505) 988-9572
Fax: (505) 988-9572
E-mail: advancetax1@cs.com

New Jersey Society of EAs
Martin Stein, EA
11 New York Blvd
Edison, NJ 08820
Phone: (732) 548-8023
Fax: (732) 548-8023
Toll Free Referral Line: (866) 652-6232
E-mail: martystax@aol.com
www.njsea.org

New York State Society of EAs
Sandra Martin, EA
15 Reitz Pkwy
Pittsford, NY 14534
Phone: (585) 381-8585
Fax: (585) 442-8252
E-mail: pats1040@aol.com
www.nyssea.org

North Carolina Society of EAs
Louis Arthur, EA
7610 Falls of The Neuse Road
Suite 100
Raleigh, NC 27615
Phone: (919) 844-6488
Fax: (919) 844-6460
E-mail: larthur@nbt-cpa.com
www.nc-sea.org

Northern New England
Society of EAs
David Landers, EA
P.O. Box 331

Rye, NH 03870
Phone: (603) 964-7177
Fax: (603) 964-9030
E-mail: taxmayvin@aol.com

Ohio State Society of EAs
Nancy Remus, EA
2901 Wexford Blvd
Stow, OH 44224
Phone: (216) 673-0463
E-mail: nremus@aol.com
www.ossea.org

Oregon Society of EAs
Peter Mar, EA
P.O. Box 23402
Eugene, OR 97402
Phone: (541) 607-9200
Fax: (541) 607-1770
E-mail: peter@helpmytaxes.com

Oklahoma Society of EAs
Leslie Armstrong, EA
2000 S. Douglas Blvd
Midwest City, OK 73130
Phone: (405) 741-0832
Fax: (405) 737-7600
E-mail: leslie@armstrongtax.com

Pennsylvania Society of EAs
George Meyers, EA
677 West DeKalb Pike
King of Prussia, PA 19406
Phone: (610) 337-2220
Fax: (610) 265-7801
E-mail: gjmea@aol.com

Rhode Island Society of EAs
D.J. Hadden, EA
27 Whipple Avenue
Westerly, RI 02891
Phone: (401) 596-6179
Fax: (401) 596-6179

South Carolina Society of EAs
Lawrence G Picard Sr., EA
400 Stratford Drive
Summerville, SC 29485-8642
Phone: (843) 871-1065
Fax: (843) 871-1332
E-mail: larrypicard@knology.net

Tennessee Society of EAs
Caryle M. Breeden, EA
7345 Middlebrook Pike
Knoxville, TN 37909
Phone: (865) 963-4274
Fax: (865) 531-1846
E-mail: tnigot2go@aol.com

Texas Society of EAs
Louis Powell, EA
408 W College Street

Carthage, TX 75633
Phone: (903) 693-7491
Fax: (903) 693-7492
E-mail: louispowel@aol.com
www.txsea.org

Utah Society of EAs
Dave Sheldon, EA
9449 Union Square #200
Sandy, UT 84070
Phone: (801) 571-2870
Fax: (801) 571-2891
E-mail: daveshel@concentric.net

Virginia Society of EAs
J. Michael Boyle, EA
P.O. Box 7246
Richmond, VA 23221
Phone: (804) 565-8055
Fax: (804) 565-8055
E-mail: j4m9b9@aol.com
www.vasea.org

VASEA Executive Director:
John M. (Mike) Hall
13208 Sherri Drive
Chester, VA 23831-4540
Phone: (804) 748-4733
Fax: (804) 748-2318
E-mail: va.sea@verizon.net

Washington State Society of EAs
Linda Shipway, EA
16605 152nd Place NE
Woodinville, WA 98072
Phone: (425) 483-2956
E-mail: linda.shipway2@verizon.net
www.wssea.org

WSSEA Administrative Office:
Mariaane Kreycik, EA
222 E Fourth Ave, Suite A
Ellensburg, WA 98926
Phone: (509) 925-6931
Fax: (509) 962-5807
E-mail: taxpro@ellensburg.com

Wisconsin Society of EAs
Diane M. Lotto, EA
200 South Washington St.
Green Bay, WI 54301
Phone: (920) 432-6466
Fax: (920) 432-5751
E-mail: dlotto@tds.net

WiSEA Executive Office
Donald Wollersheim, EA,
Executive Director
115 East Waldo Blvd.
Manitowoc, WI
Phone: (920) 684-6940

Fax: (920) 684-8208
E-mail: donw@lsol.net

International Tax Associations

International Accounting Associations:
www.taxsites.com/InternationalRegional.html

Ad Concordiam:
www.adconcordiam.net/

Canadian Payroll Association:
www.payroll.ca

Canadian Property Tax Association:
www.cpta.org

Canadian Tax Foundation:
www.ctf.ca

Canadian Taxpayers Federation:
www.taxpayer.com

Chartered Institute of Taxation - U.K.:
www.tax.org.uk

Council for International Tax Education:
www.fdta-cite.org

European-American Tax Institute:
www.e-ati.com/

European Association of Tax Law Professors:
www.eatlp.org

FSC/DISC Tax Association:
www.fdta-cite.org

Institute for Fiscal Studies - U.K.:
www.ifs.org.uk/

Institute of Taxation in Ireland:
www.taxireland.ie

Inter-American Center of Tax Administrations:
http://ciat.org

International Association of Assessing Officers:
www.iaao.org

International Fiscal Association:
www.ifa.nl

U.S. Branch:
www.ifausa.org

International Tax
Planning Association:
www.itpa.org/

North American Society of
Tax Advisors:
www.taxadvisors.com

Swedish Taxpayers
Association:
www.skattebetalarna.se

Taxation Institute of Australia:
www.taxinstitute.com.au

Taxpayers Association
of Europe:
www.taxpayers-europe.org

Taxpayers Australia:
www.taxpayer.com.au/

appendix b

Offshore Countries with Little or No Taxes

Andorra
Anguilla
Antigua and Barbuda
Aruba
Bahamas
Bahrain
Barbados
Belize
Bermuda
British Virgin Islands
Canary Islands
Cayman Islands
Cook Islands
Costa Rica
Cyprus
Dominica
Dominican Republic
Gibraltar
Grenada
Guernsey
Channel Islands Guernsey/
Sark/Alderney
Isle of Man
Jersey
Liberia
Liechtenstein
Maldives
Malta
Marshall Islands
Mauritius
Monaco
Montserrat
Nauru
Netherlands Antilles
The Dutch Antilles
Niue
Panama
Samoa or Western Samoa

San Marino
Seychelles, The Republic of Seychelles
St. Lucia
St. Kitts and Nevis, or The Principality of St. Christopher and Nevis
St. Vincent and the Grenadines, or The Republic of St. Vincent
Switzerland
Tonga
Turks and Caicos
U.S. Virgin Islands
Vanuatu

appendix C

Countries and their Religions

Catholic Nations

Nations that recognize Catholicism as the official religion include:

- Argentina
- Bolivia
- Costa Rica
- El Salvador
- Holy See
- Paraguay

Protestant Nations

Nations that recognize a form of Protestant Christianity as the official religion include:

- Vanuatu
- Samoa
- United Kingdom

Islamic Nations

Nations that recognize Islam as the official religion include:

- Afghanistan
- Algeria
- Bangladesh
- Comoros
- Libya
- Mauritania
- Morocco
- Iran
- Iraq
- Jordan
- Malaysia
- Maldives
- Oman
- Pakistan
- Saudi Arabia
- Tunisia

Buddhist Nations

Nations that recognize Buddhism as the official religion include:

- Bhutan
- Burma
- Thailand

Hindu Nations

Nations that recognize Hinduism as the official religion include:

- Nepal

appendix d

Banks by Country

Bahamian Banks

Atlantic Bank of Commerce Limited
www.firstatlanticcommerce.com
P.O. Box N8865
Nassau, N.P., The Bahamas
Phone: (242) 326-0740
Fax: (242) 325-1272
Deputy General Manager: Mrs. Hilda Knowles

BankAmerica Trust and Banking Company
www.bankofamerica.com
BankAmerica House
East Bay Street, P.O. Box N-9100
Nassau, Bahamas
Phone: (809) 393-7411
Fax: (809) 393-3030
Telex: 20 159

Bankers Trust Company
Claughton House
P.O. Box N-3234
Nassau, Bahamas
Phone: (809) 325-4107

Bank of Bahamas Limited
http://centralbankbahamas.com
50 Shirley Street, P.O. Box N-7118
Nassau, Bahamas
Phone: (809) 326-2560
Fax: (809) 325-2762

Telex: 20141 BBL

Bank of Boston Trust Company Limited
Charlotte House
P.O. Box N-3930
Nassau, Bahamas
Phone: (809) 322-8531
Telex: 20189 BOSTRUST

Bank of Nova Scotia
www.scotiabank.com/cda/content/0,,CID50_LIDen,00.html
Box N-7545 Bay Street
Nassau, Bahamas
Phone: (809) 322-4531
Fax: (809) 328-8473
E-mail: 19163288473@faxsav.com

Bahamans Offshore Accounts
http://bahamas-offshoreaccounts.com

Barclays Bank in the Bahamas
www.bahamasbanks.com
Full range of banking services

Chemical Bank & Trust Limited
www.chemicalbankmi.com
P.O. Box N-4723
Nassau N.P., The Bahamas
Phone: (242) 322-1003
Fax: (242) 326-7339
Senior Trust Officer: Mr. Michael Ranson

CIBC Trust Company
www.cibc-global.com/jur_bah_frm.html

Cititrust Bahamas
www.citibank.com
Thompson Boulevard P.O. Box -1576
Nassau, Bahamas
Phone: (809) 322-4240
Fax: (809) 325-6147
Telex: 20420

Coutts & Company Limited
www.coutts.com
P.O. Box N7788
Nassau, N.P., The Bahamas
Phone: (242) 326-0404
Fax: (242) 326-6709
Manager: Mr. James D. Graham

Darier Hentsch Private Bank & Trust Limited
www.lombardodier.com/home_en.html
P.O. Box N4983
Nassau, N.P., The Bahamas
Phone: (242) 322-2721
Fax: (242) 326-6983
Vice President: Mrs. Anna Colebrooke

Demachy Worms & Co. International
P.O. Box N3918
Nassau, N.P., The Bahamas
Phone: (242) 326-0282
Fax: (242) 326-5213
Financial Controller: Mr. Ronald W. Springle

Eastland American Bank Limited
P.O. Box N4920
Nassau, N.P., The Bahamas
Phone: (242) 325-9170
Fax: (242) 325-1002
Manager: Mr. Tyrone Fowler2

Euro-Dutch Trust Co. Limited
P.O. Box N9205
Nassau, N.P., The Bahamas
Phone: (242) 325-1033
Fax: (242) 323-7918
Managing Director: Mr. Anthony L.M. Inder Rieden

Fidinam Trust Corporation Limited
P.O. Box N9932
Nassau, N.P., The Bahamas
Phone: (242) 326-5084
Fax: (242) 328-0541
Resident Manager: Mr. Cedric B. Moss

Laurentian Bank & Trust Company Limited
www.laurentianbank.ca/en/personal_banking_services/index.html
P.O. Box N4883
Nassau, N.P., The Bahamas
Phone: (242) 326-5935
Fax: (2420 326-5871
Managing Director: Mr. E. Andre Doyon

Lloyds Bank International Private Banking
www.lloydstsb.com
P.O. Box N4843
Nassau, N.P., The Bahamas

Phone: (242) 322-8711
Fax: (242) 322-8719
Telex: 20107 BOLAM
Assistant Manager, Trust Department: Mr. Sam P. Haven

MeesPierson Limited
www.gg.meespierson.com/BankWeb
P.O. Box SS5539
Nassau, N.P., The Bahamas
Phone: (242) 393-8777
Fax: (242) 393-0582
Managing Director: Mr. Geoffrey Dyson

Montaque Securities International Limited
www.montaquesecurities.com
Saffrey Square
Bay Street & Bank Lane, 1st Floor
P.O. Box N7474
Nassau, The Bahamas
Phone: (242) 356-6133
Fax: (242) 356-6144
President & Managing Director: Owen S.M. Bethel

Morgan Trust Company of The Bahamas
www.jpmorgan.com/pages/jpmorgan/private_banking/offices
P.O. Box N4899
Nassau, N.P., The Bahamas
Phone: (242) 326-5519
Fax: (242) 326-5520
Managing Director: Mr. Andrew G Massie

Offshore Trust Banking Corporation Limited
West Bay Road, P.O. Box N7179
Nassau, Bahamas
Phone: (809) 322-4585
Telex: 20111

Rawson Trust Company Limited
P.O. Box N4465
Nassau, N.P., The Bahamas
Phone: (242) 322-7461
Fax: (242) 326-6177
Manager, Accounts: Mrs. B.M. Rolle

Royal Bank of Canada
www.rbc.com/canada

Royal Bank of Scotland (NASSAU) Limited
www.rbs.com
Box N3045, 50 Shirley Street
Nassau, Bahamas
Phone: (809) 322-4643
Fax: (809) 326-7558
E-mail: 19163267558@faxsave.com

Sand Ander Investment Bank Limited
P.O. Box N1682
Nassau, N.P., The Bahamas
Phone: (242) 322-3588
Fax: (242) 322-3585
Manager: Mrs. R. L. Symonette

The Private Trust Corporation Limited
www.privatetrustco.com

The Chase Manhattan Private Bank
www.chase.com
P.O. Box N1576
Nassau, N.P., The Bahamas
Phone: (242) 323-6811
Fax: (242) 326-8814
Unit Trust Department: Mrs. Eunice E. Smith Manager

The Citibank Private bank
www.citibank.com
P.O. Box N1576
Nassau, N.P., The Bahamas
Phone: (242) 323-3521
Fax: (242) 323-6147
Managing Director: Mr. David N. Tremblay

Thorand Trust & Management Limited
P.O. Box N3242
Nassau, N.P., The Bahamas
Phone: (242) 393-8622
Fax: (242) 393-3772
Managing Director: Mr. Robert V. Lotmore

Westpac Bank & Trust (Bahamas) Limited
www.westpac.com.au
P.O. Box N8332
Nassau, N.P., The Bahamas
Phone: (242) 328-8064
Fax: (242) 326-0067
Managing Director: Mrs. Jacqueline M. Bain

St. Lucian Banks

Bank of Novia Scotia, The
6 WM Peter Blvd
Box 301, Castries
St. Lucia
Phone: (758) 456-2100

Bank of Novia Scotia, The
Cnr Chausee Rd. & High St.
Castries, St. Lucia
Phone: (758) 452-3797

Bank of Novia Scotia, The
New Dock Rd.
Box 223, Vieux Fort
St. Lucia
Phone: (758) 454-6314

Bank of Novia Scotia, The
Rodney Bay
Gross Islet
St. Lucia
Phone: (758) 452-8805

Barclays Bank Plc.
Bridge St
Box 335
Castries, St. Lucia
Phone: (758) 456-1000

Barclays Bank Plc.
Customer Services
Castries, St. Lucia
Phone: (758) 456-1125

Barclays Bank Plc.
Operations Department
Castries, St. Lucia
Phone: (758) 456-1118

Barclays Bank Plc.
Manager Operations,
Castries, St. Lucia
Phone: (758) 456-1104

Barclays Bank Plc.
Barclays Bank Hotline
Castries, St. Lucia
Phone: (758) 451-8009

Barclays Bank Plc.
Foreign Business
Castries, St. Lucia
Phone: (758) 456-1142

Barclays Bank Plc.
Business Centre
Castries, St. Lucia
Phone: (758) 456-1008

Barclays Bank Plc.
Senior Corporate Manager

Castries, St. Lucia
Phone: (758) 456-1002

Barclays Bank Plc.
Manager Corporate Centre
Castries, St. Lucia
Phone: (758) 456-1003

Barclays Bank Plc.
Small Business Manager
Castries, St. Lucia
Phone: (758) 456-1006

Barclays Bank Plc.
Business Banker
Castries, St. Lucia
Phone: (758) 456-1123

Barclays Bank Plc.
Area Manager
Castries, St. Lucia
Phone: (758) 456-1101

Barclays Bank Plc.
Merchant Services
Castries, St. Lucia
Phone: (758) 452-2642

Barclays Bank Plc.
Manager Personal Banking
Castries, St. Lucia
Phone: (758) 452-4115

Barclays Bank Plc.
Personal Bankers
Castries, St. Lucia
Phone: (758) 456-1158

Barclays Bank Plc.
Vieux Fort
St. Lucia
Phone: (758) 454-6255

Barclays Bank Plc.
Manager
St. Lucia
Phone: (758) 454-6914

Barclays Bank Plc.
Rodney Bay Marina
Gross Islet, St. Lucia
Phone: (758) 452-9384

Barclays Bank Plc.
Insurance Broking
Barfincor, St. Lucia
Phone: (758) 453-2015

Barclays Bank Plc.
L'Anse Rd.
Castries, St. Lucia
Phone: (758) 452-4999

Barclays Bank Plc.
Apartment

Castries, St. Lucia
Phone: (758) 452-3347

Barclays Bank Plc.
Sports Club
Castries, St. Lucia
Phone: (758) 451-8259

Caribbean Banking Corporation Ltd.
Micoud St., Box 1531
Castries, St. Lucia
Phone: (758) 452-2265

Caribbean Banking Corporation Ltd.
Gablewoods Mall
Vieux Fort, St. Lucia
Phone: (758) 451-7469

Caribbean Banking Corporation Ltd.
Gablewoods Mall South
Vieux Fort, St. Lucia
Phone: (758) 454-7264

Cibe Caribbean Ltd.
Wm Peter Blvd.
Box 350
Castries, St. Lucia
Phone: (758) 456-2422

Cibe Caribbean Ltd.
Fredrick Clark St
Vieux Fort, St. Lucia
Phone: (758) 454-6262

Eastern Caribbean Central Bank
Financial Centre
Bridge St, Box 295
Castries, St. Lucia
Phone: (758) 452-7449

First Citizens Bank
www.firstcitizenstt.com
St. Lucia
Phone: (868) 623-2576

National Commercial Bank of St. Lucia Ltd.
Financial Centre Building
1 Bridge Street
Box 1860
Castries, St. Lucia
Phone: (758) 456-6000

National Commercial Bank of St. Lucia Ltd.
Bridge St. Branch
Box 1862
Castries, St. Lucia
Phone: (758) 456-6000

National Commercial Bank of
St. Lucia Ltd.
Waterfront Branch
Box 1031
Castries, St. Lucia
Phone: (758) 456-6000

National Commercial Bank of
St. Lucia Ltd.
Vieux Fort Branch
Box 261
Vieux Fort, St. Lucia
Phone: (758) 454-6327

National Commercial Bank of
St. Lucia Ltd.
Southfriere Branch
Box 243
Soufriere, St. Lucia
Phone: (758) 459-7450

National Commercial Bank of
St. Lucia Ltd.
Gros Islet Branch
Box 2046
Gros Islet, St. Lucia
Phone: (758) 450-8002

National Commercial Bank of
St. Lucia Ltd.
Bureau De Change
Hewanorra Intl. Airport
Vieux Fort, St. Lucia
Phone: (758) 454-7780

Royal Bank of Canada
Wm Peter Blvd
Box 280
Castries, St. Lucia
Phone: (758) 452-2245

Royal Bank of Canada
Audit Dept
Box 280
Castries, St. Lucia
Phone: (758) 451-9463

Royal Bank of Canada
Rodney Bay Marina
Gros Islet, St. Lucia
Phone: (758) 452-9921

Royal Bank of Canada
New Dock Rd.
Vieux Fort, St. Lucia
Phone: (758) 454-5804

Royal Bank of Canada
Business Banking Centre
Castries, St. Lucia
Phone: (758) 450-3951

St. Lucia Co-operative Ltd.

G F L Charles Airport
Castries, St. Lucia
Phone: (758) 451-8482

St. Lucia Co-operative Ltd.
JQ'S Mall
Rodney Bay, St. Lucia
Phone: (758) 452-8882

St. Lucia Co-operative Ltd.
Commercial St.
Box 342
Vieux Fort, St. Lucia
Phone: (758) 454-6213

St. Lucia Co-operative Ltd.
17 Bridge St.
Box 168
Castries, St. Lucia
Phone: (758) 455-7000

St. Lucia Co-operative Ltd.
George F L Charles Airport
Box 168
Castries, St. Lucia
Phone: (758) 451-8842

Banks of the United Kingdom

Internet & telephone banking current accounts

Cahoot Abbey National
www.cahoot.co.uk
Barclays Internet Banking
https://ibank.barclays.co.uk/olb/q/LoginMember.do

Co-op Internet Banking Smile
www.smile.co.uk

EGG
www.egg.com

Intelligent Finance
www.if.com

Lloyds TSB
www.lloydstsb.com/internet_banking.asp

Bank of Scotland
www.bosinternet.com

Virgin
www.virgin-direct.co.uk

Internet Savings Bank
www.bankofinternet.com/savings.aspx

Woolwich
www.woolwich.co.uk

High Street banks & building societies with High Street branches throughout the United Kingdom for savings & banking

Abbey National High Street Bank
www.abbeynational.co.uk

Barclays High Street
www.barclays.co.uk

Cheltenham & Gloucester
www.cheltglos.co.uk

Alliance and Leicester
www.alliance-leicester.co.uk

Bristol & West
www.bristol-west.co.uk

Bradford & Bingley
www.bradford-bingley.co.uk

Britannia
www.britannia.co.uk/home

Co-Op
www.co-operativebank.co.uk

Halifax
www.halifax.co.uk

HFC
www.hfcbank.co.uk

HSBC Midland Highstreet Bank
www.hsbc.com

Lloyds TSB
www.lloydstsb.co.uk

Nationwide
www.nationwide.co.uk

Natwest Branches
www.natwest.co.uk

Royal Bank of Scotland
www.rbs.co.uk

Portman
www.portman.co.uk

Woolwich Building Society
www.woolwich.co.uk

Yorkshire
www.ybs.co.uk

Other banks and building societies

Bank of England
www.bankofengland.co.uk

Bank of Ireland
www.bank-of-ireland.co.uk

Bank of Scotland
www.bankofscotland.co.uk

Barnsley
www.barnsley-bs.co.uk

Beverley Bank and Trust
www.thebeverlybank.com

Birmingham Midshires
www.birminghammidshires.co.uk

Cambridge
www.cambridgebs.co.uk

Capital Bank
www.capitalone.co.uk

Carter Allen
www.caterallen.co.uk

Century
www.century-bs.co.uk/

Charterhouse
www.charterhouse.co.uk

Chelsea
www.thechelsea.co.uk

Chesham
www.cheshambsoc.co.uk

Cheshire
www.thecheshire.co.uk

Citibank
http://www.citibank.co.uk

Clay Cross
www.building-societies-uk.co.uk/clay-cross-building-society.htm

Coin Co International
www.coincoplc.co.uk

Coutts
www.coutts.com

Darlington
www.darlington.co.uk

Derbyshire

www.thederbyshire.co.uk

Dudley
www.dudleybuildingsociety.co.uk

Dunfermline
www.dunfermline-bs.co.uk

Earl Shilton
www.esbs.co.uk

Ecology
www.ecology.co.uk

ECU Group
www.ecugroup.com

Express Finance
http://theexpressfinance.co.uk

First Trust Bank
www.firsttrustbank.co.uk/servletContentServer?pagename=First_Trust/GHPFirstTrust

Furness
www.furnessbs.co.uk

Hamilton
www.hdb.co.uk

Hanley Economic
www.thehanley.co.uk

Harpenden
www.harpendenbs.co.uk

Hays
www.hays-banking.co.uk

Hinckley and Rugby
www.hrbs.co.uk

ICICI Bank
www.icicibank.co.uk

Ipswich
www.ipswich-bs.co.uk

Kent Reliance
www.krbs.co.uk

Leeds & Holbeck
www.leedsbuildingsociety.co.uk

Leek
www.leek-united.co.uk

Legal & General
www.landg.com

Lombard
www.lombard.co.uk

Loughborough
www.theloughborough.co.uk

Manchester
www.themanchester.co.uk

Mansfield
www.mansfieldbs.co.uk

Market Harborough
www.mhbs.co.uk

Marsden
www.themarsden.co.uk

Melton Mowbray
www.mmbs.co.uk

Newbury
www.newbury.co.uk

Newcastle
www.newcastle.co.uk

Northern
www.nbonline.co.uk

Norwich & Peterborough
www.npbs.co.uk

Principality
www.principality.co.uk

Progressive
www.theprogressive.com

Prudential
www.pru.co.uk

Saffron Waldon Herts
www.swhebs.co.uk

Scarborough
www.scarboroughbs.co.uk

Scottish
www.scottishbldgsoc.co.uk

Shepshed
www.theshepshed.co.uk

Skipton
www.skipton.co.uk

Spanish/Gibraltar
www.npbs-gibraltar.co.uk

Stafford Railway
www.srbs.co.uk

Standard Bank
www.sbl.co.uk

Standard Chartered
www.stanchart.com

Standard Life
www.standardlifebank.com

Stroud & Swindon
www.stroudandswindon.co.uk

Swansea
www.swansea-bs.co.uk

Teachers
www.teachersbs.co.uk

Tridos
www.triodos.co.uk

Swiss Banks

A &A Actienbank
ABB Export Bank
ABN AMRO Bank (Schweiz)
ABN AMRO Bank N.V. Amsterdam
AIG Private Bank Ltd.
ANZ Grindlays Bank Ltd.
AP Anlage & Privatbank AG Bach
Aargauische Kantonalbank
Adler & Co. AG
Alternative Bank ABD
Amas Bank (Switzerland) Ltd.
American Express Bank (Switzerland)
Amtsersparniskasse Oberhasli
Amtsersparniskasse Schwarzenbu
Amtsersparniskasse Thun
Anker Bank
Appezeller Kantonalbank
Arab Bank (Switzerland) Ltd.
Aramd von Ernst & Cie. AG
Artesia (Suisse) SA
Arzi Bank AG
Atlantic Vermogensverwaltungsbank
BB Bank Belp
BBVA Privanza Bank (Switzerland) Ltd.
BDL Banco di Lugano
BEKB BCBE
BFC Banque Financiere de la Cite
BGG Banque Genevoise de Gestion
BHF Bannk (Schweiz) AG
BLP Banque de Oirtefeyukkes
BNP Paribas (Suisse) SA
BS Bank Schaffhausen
BSI SA
BZ Bank Aktiengesellschaft
Banca Arner SA

Banca Commerciale Italiana (Switzerland)
Banca Commerciale Lugano
Banca Euromobiliare (Suisse) SA
Banca Monte Paschi (Suisse) SA
Banca Popolare di Sondrio (Suisse) SA
Banca Privata Edmond de Rothchild Lugano SA
Banca Unione di Credito
Banca del Ceresio SA
Banca del Gottardo
Banca del Sempione
Banca dello Stato del Cantone Ticino
Banca di Credito e Commercio (BANKREDIT)
Banco Espirito Santo SA
Banco Mercantil (Schweiz) AG
Banco Santander Cenrtal Hispano (Suiza) SA
Bank Adamas AG
Bank Austria Cerditanstalt (Schweiz) AG
Bank Butschwil
Bank CIAL (Schweiz)
Bank Coop
Bank EEK
Bank Ehinger & Cie.
Bank Eschenback
Bank Hapoalim (Schweiz) AG
Bank Hofman AG
Bank Hugh Kahn & Co. AG
Bank J. Vontobel & Co. AG
Bank Jacob Safra (Schweiz) AG
Bank Julius Bar & Co. AG
Bank Leerau
Bank Leu AG
Bank Leumi le-Israel (Schweiz)
Bank Linth
Bank Morgan Stanley AG
Bank Sal. Oppenheim Jr. & Cie.
Bank Sprasin & Cie.
Bank Sparhafen Zurich
Bank Thorbecke AG
Bank Wartau-Sevelen
Bank am Bellvue
Bank for International Settlements
Bank fur Handle & Effekten
Bank im Thal
Bank in Gossau
Bank in Huttwil
Bank in Langnau AG
Bank in Zuzwil
Bank of America National Association
Bank of New York – Inter-maritime Bank

Bank of Tokyo – Mitsubishi (Schweiz) AG
Bank von Ernst & Cie AG
Banque Alerienne du Commerce Exterieur SA
Banque Audi (Suisse) SA
Banque Banorient (Suisse)
Banque Baring Brothers (Suisse) SA
Banque Bonhote & Cie SA
Banque Bruxelles Lambert (Suisse) SA
Banque CAI Caisse Alfa Banques
Banque Cantonale Neuchateloise
Banque Cantonale Vaudoise
Banque Cantonale de Fribourg
Banque Cantonale de Geneve
Banque Cantonale du Jura
Banque Cantonale du Valais
Banque Degroof Luxembourg SA
Banque Diamantaire Anversoise (Suisse) SA
Banque Edourad Constant SA
Banque Franck SA
Banque Francaise de l'Orient (Suisse) SA
Banque Galland & Cie SA
Banque General du Luxembourg (Suisse) SA
Banque International de Commerce BRED
Banque Ippa & Associates, Luxembourg
Banque Jenni & Cie. SA
Banque Jurassienne d'Epargne et de Credit
Banque Labouchere SA
Banque MeesPierson Gonet SA
Banque Multi Commercials
Banque Nationale de Paris (Suisse) SA
Banque Notz Stucki SA
Banque Pasche SA
Banque Piguet & Cie. SA
Banque Privee Edmond de Rothschild SA
Banque SCS Alliance SA
Banque Syz & Co. SA
Banque Tardy de Watteville & Cie. SA
Banque Thaler
Banque Unexim (Suisse) SA
Banque Vontobel Geneve SA
Banque Worms (Geneve) SA
Banque de Camondo (Suisse) SA
Banque de Commerce et de Placements SA

Banque de Depots et de Gestion
Banque de Gestion Financiere BAGEFI
Banque de Patrimoines Prives Geneve BPG SA
Bantleon Bank AG
Barclays Bank (Suisse) SA
Basellandschafliche Kantonalbank
Banque Cantonale de Bale
Baumann & Cie.
Bayeriche Landesbank (Schweiz) AG
Benrnberg Bank (Schweiz) A
Bezirks-Sparkasse Dielsdorf
Bezirkskasse Laufen
Bezirkssparkasse Uster
Biene - Bank im Rheintal
Bordier & Cie.
Burgerliche Ersparniskasse Bern
C.I.M.Banque
CBG Banca Privata Lugano SA
CBG Compagnie Bancaire Geneve
Caisse d'Epargne Le Cret
Caisse d'Epargne d'Aubonne
Caisse d'Epargne de Nyon
Caisse d'Epargne de Perz
Caisse d'Epargne de Siviriez
Caisse d'Epargne de Vuisternenr-devant-Romont
Caisse d'Epargne de la Ville de Fribourg
Caisse d'Epargne du District de Cossonay
Caisse d'Epargne du District de Courtelary
Cassie d'Epargne du District de Vevey
Caisse d'Epargne et de Credit Mutuel de Chermignon
Caisse d'Epargne et de Pervoyance d'Yverdon-les-Bains SA
Caisse d'Epargne et de Pervoyance de Lausanne
Canto Consulting
Cantrade Privatbank AG
Citibank (Switzerland)
Citibank N.A.
Clariden Bank
Commerzbank (Schweiz)
Compagnie Bancaire Espirito Santo SA
Corner Banca SA
Cosba Private Banking SA
Coutts & Co. AG
Credit Suisse
Credit Suisse First Boston

Credit Agricole Indosuez (Suisse) SA
Credit Commercial de France (Suisse)
Credit Lyonnais (Suisse)
Credit Mutuel de la Vallee SA
DC Bank Debosito-Cassa der Stadt Bern
Dai-Ichi Kangyo Bank
Deka (Swiss) Privatbank
Deutsche Bank (Schweiz)
Deutsche Bank (Suisse)
Dexia Privatbank
Direkt Anlage Bank
Discount Bank and Trust Company
Dominick Company AG
Dresdner Bank (Schweiz) AG
Dreyfus Sohne & Cie.
E. Gutzwiller & Cie. AG
EB Entlebucher Bank
EFG Bank European Financial Group
EFG Private Bank
Ersparniskasse Breinz
Ersparnisanstalt Oberuzwil
Ersparnisanstalt Unterwasser
Ersparnisanstalt der Stadt St. Gallen
Ersparniskasseschaft Kuttigen Kuttigen
•Ersparniskasse Affoltern i.E.
Ersparniskasse Durrenroth
Ersparniskasse Erlinsbach
Ersparniskasse Murten
Ersparniskasse Rueggisberg
Ersparniskasse Schaffhausen
Ersparniskasse Speicher
Ersparniskasse Wyssachen-Eriswil
Ersparniskasse des Amts-bezirks Interlanke
Eurasco Bank AG
F. van Lanschot Bankiers
FCE Bank
FIBI Bank
FTI Banque Fiduciary Trust
Ferrier Lullin & Cie.
Finansbank (Suisse)
Finter Bank
Freie Gemeinschaftsbank BCL
GE Capital Bank
GRB Garner Kantonalbank
Goldman Sachs & Co.
Gonet & Cie.
Graubunder Kantonalbank
HSBC Bank Middle East
HSBC Guyerzeller Bank AG
HSBC Republic Bank (Suisse) SA
HYPOSWISS Schweizerische Hypotheken

Habib Bank AG
Habibsons Bank Limited
Handelsfinaz CCF Bank
Helaba (Schweiz) Landesbank
Hessen-Thuringen
Hentsch Henschoz & Cie.
Hottiner & Cie.
Hypothekarbank Lenzburg
IBI Bank
IBZ Bank
ING Bank N.V.
ING Baring Private Bank
IRB Interregiobank
Instinet (Schweiz) A
Investec Bank (Switzerland)
J.P. Morgan (Suisse) SA
Jyske Bank
KGS Sensebank
Kanz Bank
Kreditebank
LT Bank in Liechtenstein
La Roch & Co. Banquiers
Landolt & Cie. Banquiers
Lavoro Bank AG
Leihkasse Stammheim
Liechtensteinische Landesbank
Lienhardt & Partner Privatbank Zurich
Lloyds TSB Bank plc
Lombard Odier Darier
Hentsch & Cie.
Luzerner Kantonalbank
Luzerner Regiobank AG
M.M. Warburg Bank
MIGROSBANK
Maerki, Baumann & Co.
Marcurad Cook & Cie. SA
MediBank
Merrill Lynch Bank
Merrill Lynch Capital Markets
Mirabaud & Cie.
Mitsubishi Tokyo Wealth
Management
Mizuho Bank
Morgan Guaranty Trust Company of New York
Morval & Cie. SA
Mourgue d'Algue & Cie.
National Bank of Kuwait
Neue Aargauer Bank
Nidwalder Kantonalbank
Nomura Bank
Nordea Bank S.A.
Nordfinanz Bank Zurich
OZ Bankers AG
Obersimmentalische
Volksbank
Obwalder Kantonalbank
PBS Privat Bank AG
PKB Privatbank AG
Pictet & Cie.
Privatbank Bellerive AG

Privatbank IHAG Zurich AG
Privatbank Vermag AG
Privatbank Von Graffenreied AG
RBA Zentralbank
Rabo Robeco Bank
Rahn & Bodmer
Redsafe Bank
Regiobank Solothurn
Reichmuth & Co.
Reisebank AG
Robert Fleming (Switzerland)
Rothschild Bank AG
Royal Bank of Canada
Russische Kommerzial Bank
RUd, Blass, & Cie.
SB Saanen Bank
SEB Private Bank
SG Ruegg Bank
SIS AGSegaIntersettle
Sanwa Bank
Schaffhauser Kantonalbank
Schmidt Bank
Schorder &Co. Bank
Schweizer Verband der Raiffeisenbanken
Schweizerische Hypotheken
Schweizerische Nationalbank
Schweizerische Schiffshyphothenkenbank
Scwyzer Kantonalbank
Scobag AG
Skandia Bank
Societa Bancaria Ticinese
Societe Generale
Solothurner Bank SoBa
Spar + Leihkasse Frutigen
Spar + Leihkasse Gurbetal
Spar und Leihkasse Balgach
Spar und Leihkasse Bucheggberg
Spar und Leihkasse Kaltbrunn
Spar und Leihkasse Kirchberg (SG)
Spar und Leihkasse Leuk und Umgebung
Spar und Leihkasse Madiswil
Spar und Leihkasse Melchnau
Spar und Leihkasse Munsingen
Spar und Leihkasse Rebstein
Spar und Leihkasse Riggisberg
Spar und Leihkasse Steffisburg
Spar und Leihkasse Sumiswalkd
Spar und Leihkasse Thayngen
Spar und Liehkasse Wynigen
Sparcassa 1816
Spargenossenschft Mosnang
Sparkasse Engleberg
Sparkasse Horgen
Sparkasse Kusnacht ZH

Sparkasse Oberriet
Sparkasse Oftingen
Sparkasse Schwyz
Sparkasse Thalwil
Sparkasse Trogen
Sparkasse Wiesendangen
Sparkasse Zurcher Oberland
Sparkasse des Sensebezirks
St. Gallische Creditanstalt
St. Gallische Kantonalbank
Swissfirst Bank AG
Swissquote Bank
Synthesis Bank
Tempus Privatbank AG
The Chase Manhattan Private Bank (Switzerland)
Thurgauer Kantonalbank
Tokai Bank (Schweiz) AG
Trafina Privatbank AG
Triba Partner Bank
UBS AG
UBS Card Center AG
UEB United European Bank
UniCredit (Suisse) Bank SA
Unibank SA
Union Bancaire Privee
Untied Bank AG
United Mizrahi Bank (Schweiz) AG
Urner Kantonalbank
VP Bank (Schweiz) AG
Valiant Bank
Valiant Privatbank
Volksbank Bodensee AG
Vorarlberger Landes und Hypothekenbank AG
WIR Bank
Welin & Co. Privatbankiers
Westdeutsche Landesbank (Schweiz) AG
ZLB Zurcher Landbank
Zuger Kantonalbank
Zurcher Kantonalbank
Zurich Invest bank AG

bibliography

"Aliens and U. S. Citizens Living Abroad: Canadian and U. S. Tax Issues." IRS.GOV. June 2008. <**www.irs.gov/faqs/faq13.html**>.

"Best websites for Embassies, Visa, Passports and Work Permits." EXPATRIATES.com. June 2008. <**www.transitionsabroad.com/nav-pages/links/bestembassies.shtml**>.

"Building Safety." EMERGEDV. June 2008. <**www.emergedv.com/safety.html**>.

Charrett, Sheldon, *The Modern Identify Changer,* Paladin Press, Boulder, Colorado, 2004.

"Country Networks." EXPATEXCHANGE.com. May 2008. <**www.expatexchange.com/nets.cfm**>.

"Earn Up to $87,600 Oversees Tax-Free." INTERNATIONALLIVING.com. July 2008. <**www.internationalliving.com/publications/expat_advice/taxes**>.

EARTHCLASSMAIL.com. June 2008. <**www.earthclassmail.com**>.

"Employment Opportunities." EMPLOYMENTOFFICE.NET. June 2008. <**www.employmentoffice.net**>.

"Expats Guide to Moving Abroad." EXPATFORUM.com. June 2008. **<www.expatforum.com>**.

"Facial Recognition." World of Forensic Science. Thomson Gale. 2005. Encyclopedia.com. 30 Dec. 2009 **<www.encyclopedia.com/searchresults.aspx?q=Facial+Recognition>**.

"Money Matters for Expatriates and Travelers Abroad." EXPATRIATES.com. May 2008. **<www.transitionsabroad.com/listings/living/resources/financialmatters.shtm>**.

"Health, Safety and Insurance for Travelers and Expatriates Abroad." EXPATRIATES.com. May 2008. **<www.transitionsabroad.com/listings/living/resources/healthandsafety.shtml>**.

"How to Find What you Want." www.clickflatshare.com. May 2008. **<www.ma.hw.ac.uk/~katie/find.htm>**.

"If You're A Wanted Fugitive in the US And You Blog, Maybe Don't Mention Plans to Travel To A US Territory." TECHDIRT.com. June 2008. **<www.techdirt.com/articles/20080229/080250385.shtml>**

"Immigrating to Canada." CIC.GC.CA. April 2008. **<www.cic.gc.ca/english/immigrate/index.asp>**.

"Income Tax Refunds for People Living Abroad." JOBSABROAD.com. July 2008. **<www.jobsabroad.com/search.cfm>**.

"International Spotlight." ENDABUSE.org **<http://endabuse.org/programs/display.php3?DocID=190>**.

Luna, J. J., *How To Be invisible,* St. Martin's Press, New York, 2004.

JOBPILOT.com. June 2008. **<www.jobsabroad.com/search.cfm>**.

"Life on the "QT" or "PT" - All in the Quest to Retain Your Privacy". EXPATWORLD.net. June 2008. **<www.expatworld.net/downloads/index.html>**.

"Links Directory." EXPATNETWORK.com. July 2008. **<www.expat-network.com/?ID=96>**.

"Living Abroad Advisor." June 2008. TRANSITIONSABROAD.com. **<www.transitionsabroad.com/listings/living/index.shtml#living_abroad_advisor>**.

"Living in Europe." EXPATICA.COM. May 2008. **<www.expatica.com/hr/story/Moscow-most-expensive-city-for-expats.html>**.

"Missing Persons in Australia." National Missing Persons Coordination Centre. December 2009. **<www.missingpersons.gov.au/research/reports/missing-persons-australia.aspx>**.

"Missing Persons and Unidentified Remains: The Nation's Silent Mass Disaster". National Institute of Justice. December 2009. **<www.ojp.usdoj.gov/nij/journals/256/missing-persons.html>**.

"New Start. New Opportunities. New Zealand." IMMIGRATION.GOVT.NZ, July 2008. **<www.immigration.govt.nz/nzopportunities/>**.

Pankau, Edmund J, *Hide Your Assets And Disappear,* HarperCollins Publishers, New York, 2000.

"People Search and Public Information." ZABASEARCH.COM. July 2008. **<www.zabasearch.com>**.

"Profiles of International Employers." INTERNATIONALJOBS.org . June 2008. **< www.internationaljobs.org>**.

"Protecting Your Privacy." JOB-HUNT.org. April 2008. <www.job-hunt.org/ privacy.shtml>.

"Restart Your Life Overseas." ESCAPEARTIST.com. April 2008. **<www.escapeartist.com/Living_Overseas/>**.

"Security Focus." CTCNET. May 2008. **<www.ctcnet.org/resources>**.

"Smart Dossiers." TECHDIRT.com. June 2008. **<www.techdirt.com/smart-dossiers.php>**.

"Social Security Benefits while Living Abroad." SSA.GOV. April 2008. **<http://search.ssa.gov>**.

"Teaching Competencies for the International Educator:" ECIS.org. May 2008. **<www.internationalteachercertificate.com>**.

"Ten dangerous claims about smart phone security." Computerworld - News, Education & Headlines - Security, Storage & Networking - Information on Hardware, Software for Laptops & Desktops. Web. 29 Dec. 2009. **<www.computerworld.com/s/article/9014118/Ten_dangerous_claims_about_smart_phone_security?taxonomyId=17&pageNumber=1>**.

"The Legal Route." EXPATRIATECAFE.com. July 2008. **<www.expatriatecafe.com/index.php?option=articles&task=viewarticle&artid=4&Itemid=3>**.

"The Plain Truth About Living in Mexico." TravelTourism.com/lasr.net. July 2008 **<www.traveltotourism.com/travelarticles.php?The+Plain+Truth+about+Living+in+Mexico&ID=325>**

TIPTOP.JOB.com. June 2008. **<www.thegloballife.net/>**.

Wilson, B., *Cover Your Tracks Without Changing Your Identify,* Paladin Press, Boulder, Colorado, 2003.

biography

David Wilkening is a former newspaperman who has worked in Chicago, Detroit, Washington, D.C., and Orlando. He also was involved as an advisor and consultant in politics before becoming a freelance writer who specializes in travel and business real estate. He has written numerous travel articles and guides. He lives in Orlando and collaborates at times with his wife, Suzanne, who is also a writer.

index

A

B

C

D

E

F

G

H

I

S

T

U

V

W